Access to Modern European Studies

John Pratten
and
David Stevenson

TUDOR

First published in Great Britain in 1996 by
Tudor Business Publishing Ltd.
Sole distributors worldwide, Hodder and Stoughton (Publishers) Ltd,
338 Euston Road London NW1 3BH

A CIP catalogue record for this book is available from the British Library

ISBN 1 872807 61 5

1 2 3 4 5   95 96 97 98 99

Typeset by Deltatype Ltd, Ellesmere Port, Cheshire
Printed and bound by Athenaeum Press, Ltd.,
Gateshead, Tyne & Wear.

Contents

To Irene and Malcolm with grateful thanks for their patience, support and understanding

To Amanda, Zoë and Gregory for everything

Introduction

This book is aimed principally at HND and other undergraduates in the field of Business Studies. An increasing number of institutions now teach European Studies as part of their Business Studies courses. This reflects the growing impact of the EU on the business environment in the UK.

There are already many sound European Studies works, though most of these cater for the student of Politics, Government or History. For Business Studies undergraduates, books of this type are probably too specialised to be of real value. While European Studies books do exist which are aimed at Business Studies undergraduates, the choice appears rather limited.

This volume therefore caters for the student following European Studies as part of a Business Studies qualification. There is, therefore, little need for analysis of theoretical concepts. Instead it concentrates on practicalities.

Information is given on each EU member in the form of basic economic data. Chapters are also devoted to marketing in the EU and to the business climate in each of the countries under consideration. The book also has a brief history of European integration, a study of the major EU and non-EU institutions in Europe and a chapter on the UK and Europe. The final chapter is devoted to the future.

The maps used in the text show geographical locations of countries in the EU and do not show all of the places mentioned in the text. The student may like to refer to a more detailed atlas for this purpose.

Activities

At the end of each chapter, there is a suggested activity. The intention is to provide the students with a task that they can undertake either in the classroom, in the library, or outside the institution.

The common theme of the activities is the collection of information relating to a country not dealt with in the book. It may be best that such a country is within Europe, or at least is a potential member of the European Union. This could include islands such as Cyprus and Malta, and might extend to Turkey and Israel.

The problem of assignments such as this is a shortage of source material. Before allowing any student to select a country, it is advisable to make sure that certain basic texts are available. These could be:

- Department of Trade and Industry Export Publications relating to the particular country
- the Royal Mail International Travel Guide
- a good, up-to-date Atlas
- back copies of the *Economist* and the *Financial Times* containing relevant material
- The Economist Diary
- the Embassies of the various countries are happy to provide information, as are the Tourist Boards.

The international divisions of the main clearing banks are another potential source of data. As the activities become more difficult in terms of sources, it may be necessary to offer increasing guidance, but it is a worthwhile part of such an activity that students observe that some information is extremely difficult to collect.

Common Abbreviations

ACP	–	African, Caribbean and Pacific (States)
BENELUX	–	Belgium, Netherlands, Luxembourg
BERD	–	European Bank for Reconstruction and Development (from French)
BRITE	–	Basic Research in Industrial Technology in Europe
CAP	–	Common Agricultural Policy
CCP	–	Common Commercial Policy
CCT	–	Common Customs Tariff
CET	–	Common External Tariff
CFP	–	Common Fisheries Policy
CIS	–	Commonwealth of Independent States
CMEA	–	Council for Mutual Economic Assistance (COMECON)
COMETT	–	Community Programme in Education and Training in Technology
COREPER	–	Committee of Permanent Representatives (from French)
COST	–	Co-operation on Science and Technology
CPSU	–	Communist Party of the Soviet Union
DB	–	Deutsche Bundesbahn (German Federal Railways)
DG	–	Directorate-General (of European Commission)
EC	–	European Community
ECHR	–	European Court of Human Rights
ECJ	–	European Court of Justice
ECOFIN	–	Economics and Financial Council
ECOSOC	–	Economic and Social Committee
ECSU	–	European Coal and Steel Community
ECU	–	European Currency Unit
EDC	–	European Defence Community

EDF	–	European Development Fund
EEA	–	European Economic Area
EEC	–	European Economic Community
EEZ	–	European Economic Zone
EFTA	–	European Free Trade Association
EIB	–	European Investment Bank
EMCF	–	European Monetary Co-operation Fund
EMF	–	European Monetary Fund
EMS	–	European Monetary System
EMU	–	Economic and Monetary Union
EP	–	European Parliament
EPC	–	European Political Co-operation OR European Political Community
ERDF	–	European Regional Development Fund
ERM	–	Exchange Rate Mechanism (or EMS)
ESC	–	Economic and Social Committee
ESCB	–	European System of Central Banks
ESPRIT	–	European Research and Development in Information Technology
EU	–	European Union
EUA	–	European Unit of Account
EURATOM	–	European Atomic Energy Authority
FTA	–	Free Trade Area
GATT	–	General Agreement on Tariffs and Trade
GDP	–	Gross Domestic Product
GNP	–	Gross National Product
IATA	–	International Air Transport Association
IBRD	–	International Bank for Reconstruction and Development (World Bank)
LDC	–	Less Developed Country
MCA	–	Monetary Compensation Account
MEP	–	Member of the European Parliament
MFA	–	Multi-Fibre Agreement
MFN	–	Most Favoured National
NAFTA	–	North American Free Trade Area
NATO	–	North Atlantic Treaty Organisation
NFU	–	National Farmers' Union
NIC	–	Newly Industrialised Country
OECD	–	Organisation for Economic Co-operation and Development
OEEC	–	Organisation for European Economic Cooperation
OOP	–	Office for Official Publications (of EU)
OPEC	–	Organisation of Petroleum Exporting Countries
PR	–	Proportional Representation

R&D	–	Research and Development
SAD	–	Single Administrative Document
SAP	–	Social Action Programme
SEA	–	Single European Act
SEM	–	Single European Market
STV	–	Single Transferable Vote
UA	–	Unit of Account
UN	–	United Nations
UNO	–	United Nations Organisation
VAT	–	Value Added Tax
VER	–	Voluntary Export Restraint

Chapter One

The Countries of the European Union

Aims of this chapter

☐ To provide basic geographic, demographic, industrial and commercial information on the countries of Western Europe

☐ To highlight the distinctive features of the respective countries

☐ To allow students to appreciate the differences which exist within Western Europe

Although the process of integration has eroded divisions between countries, Europe remains economically, culturally and politically diverse. Differences affect the business environment and influence the conditions under which businesses operate, and also the ways in which people behave.

All the countries discussed are members of the European Union, except Iceland, Liechtenstein, Norway and Switzerland. Much of the material is statistical. Figures have been rounded up or down as appropriate. Every effort has been made to ensure accuracy, but other sources may offer alternative data.

For each country, the chapter includes:

- a map
- the geographical location, including land borders and coastline where appropriate, size and climatic type
- the population, the languages spoken, the main religions, and the main towns and cities

- a brief account of the system of government, including the distribution of power
- the main industries
- the main goods that are imported and exported, together with the trading partners
- details of the transport system including roads, railways, airports and, where appropriate, waterways.

Austria

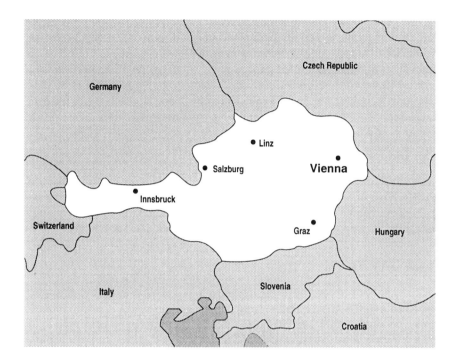

Geography

Austria is landlocked, and borders Germany, the Czech Republic, Slovakia, Hungary, Slovenia, Italy, Liechtenstein and Switzerland. Its major features include mountains and lakes as well as the valley of the River Danube. Austria covers an area of 84,000 square kilometres (32,500 square miles), of which 20% is cultivated, 26% meadows and pastures, 38% forest and 1% inland water. Austria has few natural resources. The climate is moderate continental, with warm, sunny summers and sufficient snow for winter sports.

Population

Austria has a population of almost eight million and a density of 93 per square kilometre. The capital is Vienna with a population of one and a half million. Other major cities include Graz, Linz, Salzburg and Innsbruck. The official language is German, but there are strong regional dialects. 89% of the population is Roman Catholic and 6% Protestant.

System of government

Austria is a federal republic. Its parliament has two chambers, which sit in Vienna. The National Council (Nationalrat) is directly elected by proportional representation and the Federal Council (Bundesrat) is elected by the provincial assemblies. The Federal President, who is directly elected, is head of state and acts on the advice of the Council of Ministers led by a Federal Chancellor responsible to the Nationalrat. The country is divided into nine provinces (Länder) including the Capital, each with its own Assembly.

Main industries

Agriculture, including forestry, fishing and hunting, contributes less than 3% of GDP, but produces 90% of Austria's food requirements. Manufacturing contributes over 30% of GDP. The main sectors are machinery, metals, food products, wood and paper. Tourism is also significant.

Trade

Austria's main trading partners are Germany, Italy, France and the UK. The main exports are machinery and transport equipment, basic manufactures and crude materials. Imports include chemicals, mineral fuels and energy, machinery and transport equipment.

Transport system

Austria has an excellent, well-maintained road system. There are tolls on some roads. Bus and coach services operate throughout the country. Austrian Federal Railways operate an efficient rail network, with regular inter-city and international expresses as well as good connecting services elsewhere. The main international airport is at Vienna, but some international flights use Graz, Innsbruck, Salzburg, Klagenfurt and Linz. There are regular domestic flights. In the summer, there are regular passenger services along the Danube and on the lakes, and cruises along the Danube to the Black Sea.

Belgium

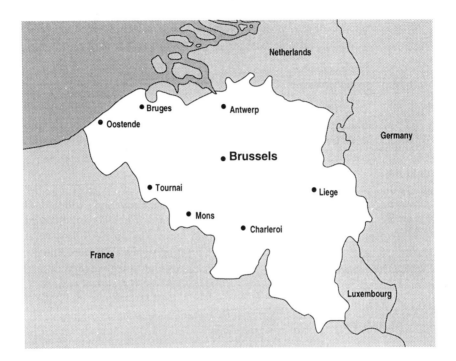

Geography

The north and west of the country is a plain, while the south and east contain hills and valleys. It borders France, Germany, the Netherlands and Luxembourg. The coastline is short, measuring only 64 kilometres (40 miles). Belgium is one of the smallest countries in Europe, with a land area of 30,500 square kilometres (11,800 square miles), of which 28% is cultivated, 25% meadow and pasture, and 20% forest. The climate is temperate, with mild winters and pleasant summers.

Population

Belgium has a population of about ten million, of whom 55% are Flemish, 33% Walloon, 12% mixed or other. Approximately 35% of the people live in the major industrial areas, and the country as a whole has the very high population density of 328 per square kilometre. The capital, Brussels, has a population of almost one million. Other major cities include Antwerp, Ghent, Charleroi, Liège and Bruges. The languages spoken in Belgium are

Flemish, French and German. Flemish is used in Flanders, which contains about 58% of the total population, while Wallonia which has about 33% of the population speaks French, and German is used in the area bordering Germany. The Brussels region employs both Flemish and French. Most Belgians are Roman Catholic, with small Protestant and Jewish minorities.

System of government

Belgium is a constitutional monarchy, with a Chamber of Deputies elected by proportional representation, and a Senate which is partly elected and partly appointed. In 1989, Belgium became a federal state, in an attempt to solve the endemic friction between the Dutch and French speaking communities. There are three Community Councils, responsible for social and cultural matters, and Regional Councils to deal with planning, the environment, energy and transport. There are nine Provinces, which deal with public order, education, health and public works. Each is administered by a governor appointed by the monarch, and has elected provincial Councils. The Provinces are made up of Communes, which have councils. Belgium has a large number of political parties, so coalition governments are usual.

Main industries

Manufacturing accounts for about 28%, agriculture 3% and financial and other business and insurance services and real estate industries nearly 9% of the employed workforce.

Trade

Belgium's main trading partners are Germany, France, the Netherlands and the UK. Exports are related to the imports. Manufactured products including diamonds, machinery, transport equipment, chemicals, clothing and food are exported, and imports include machinery and transport equipment, chemicals, gems, food and animals.

Transport system

There are over 900 miles of toll-free motorways, 6,000 miles of main roads, and over 30,000 miles of secondary roads. As there are over four million vehicles, road usage is heavy. Belgian National Railways operate a dense rail network, with over 2,000 miles of lines regularly serving all parts of the country. A high-speed link to the Channel Tunnel is under construction. Brussels National, which has a direct rail link to the city centre, is Belgium's main international airport, but there are others at Antwerp, Ostend, Liège and Charleroi. The principal harbours are Antwerp, Zeebrugge and

Ostend (Oostende), and the main inland ports are Brussels, Ghent, Liège and Charleroi. Antwerp is one of the largest ports in Europe with extensive container facilities and a huge refinery complex. There is an extensive canal system linking the industrial regions.

Denmark

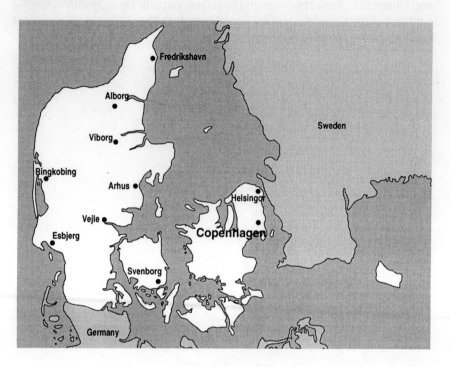

Geography

Denmark is the smallest of the Scandinavian countries, covering an area of 43,000 square kilometres (16,600 square miles), excluding Greenland and the Faroes. Of this, 64% is arable, 8% meadows and pastures and 11% forest. Virtually all of the country is flat. There are a large number of lakes and islands. The Danish coastline measures 3,380 kilometres (2,100 miles). Denmark's only land border is with Germany. The climate is temperate with high rainfall. Summer is short, winter frosty, spring and autumn mild.

Population

Denmark has a population of just over five million, nearly all of whom live in Denmark itself. The density is 120 per square kilometre. Copenhagen is the country's capital, as well as being the political and commercial centre. It has a population of about half a million. Other major cities include Aarhus (Arhus), Odense, Aalborg (Alborg) and Esbjerg. The official language is

Danish with a small German-speaking minority in the south. Most Danes are Evangelical Lutheran.

System of government

Denmark is a constitutional monarchy, with a single chamber of Parliament (Folketing) in which members from the Faroe Islands and Greenland also sit. However, these two have home rule and have not joined the EU. They have their own assemblies, and send representatives to the Danish Parliament, which is responsible for their defence and foreign policies. There are many political parties, and governments are often coalitions. There is a consensus approach to decision making, which can result in inertia, and can cause frustration in the business community.

Main industries

Denmark is an efficient industrial nation, with important agriculture, transport and energy sectors. By 1992, Denmark was self sufficient in oil and gas. Electricity is produced from imported coal, but the use of natural gas is increasing. Nuclear energy is not used. Shipping is Denmark's third largest export earner, utilising a large and modern merchant fleet, composed of about one-third tankers, three-fifths cargo carriers and the rest passenger vessels. Most of the fleet is engaged in trade outside the country. About two-thirds of agricultural production is exported, with Britain as one of Denmark's largest markets. Food processing accounts for almost one-third of all industrial sales in Denmark and there is a large fish processing industry.

Trade

Denmark's main trading partners are Germany, Sweden, the UK and the USA. The main exports are food and food products, metal goods, electronics, chemicals and paper. Imports include raw materials and machinery.

Transport system

The road system is good. Danish State Railways operate a partially-electrified network of express services between the main centres, supplemented by connecting bus services in rural areas. There are ferries from Denmark to neighbouring countries, and passenger and car ferries link the islands to each other and the mainland. Copenhagen has an international airport, and there are many domestic airports.

Finland

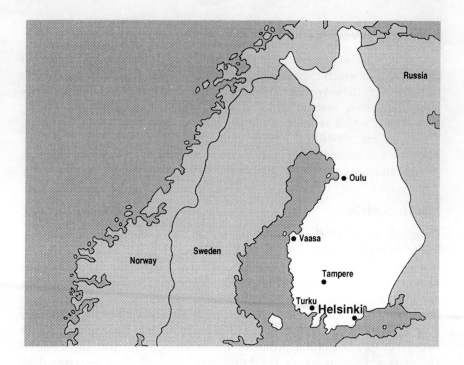

Geography

About one-third of the country is north of the Arctic Circle. It has about 30,000 off-shore islands and 62,000 inland lakes, which themselves contain a further 98,000 islands. Finland covers an area of about 338,000 square kilometres (130,000 square miles) of which 8% is arable, 65% forest and 10% lake. The coastline is 1,126 kilometres (700 miles) in length. The country boarders Norway, Sweden and Russia. The climate is continental, being warm in summer and very cold in winter, varying with latitude.

Population

Finland is sparsely populated, with about five million people, giving it a density of almost 15 per square kilometre. The capital, Helsinki, has a population of around half a million. Other major cities include Tampere and Turku. 94% of the population speak Finnish. Most of the remainder speak Swedish, with some Lapp in the North. 90% of the population are members of the Evangelical Lutheran National Church (state supported), with other Christian minorities, and some Jews and Moslems.

System of government

Finland is a republic. The single chamber Parliament (Eduskunta) is elected by proportional representation. There is a wide variety of political parties, so coalition governments are common. The President is elected and appoints a Prime Minister and a Council of State (Cabinet), responsible to the Eduskunta. The country is divided into 12 Provinces, 443 Communes and 78 Towns, all of which have some powers.

Main industries

Agriculture, forestry, fishing and hunting together account for over 3% of GDP. Industry contributes nearly 25%, construction 9%, trade, restaurants and hotels 11%, transport and communication 8%, finance and insurance 4%, other private services 19%, producers of government services 17%. The main industries in order of importance are metal and engineering, forestry, food and chemicals.

Trade

Finland's main trade partners are Germany and Sweden. The main exports include paper and paper products, wood and pulp, metal and engineering products. Imports include machinery and transport equipment, mineral fuels, chemicals and consumer goods.

Transport system

The large size of the country, the small population and the harsh winters combine to necessitate an efficient transport system. There is a dense network of roads, but only short stretches of motorways. The rest is well surfaced, with many snow ploughs to ensure that the main roads are always passable in winter. There is a very good bus network and local transport systems are good. Express rail services connect Helsinki to the main towns. Trains are comfortable and punctual. The gauge is different to that used in most of Western Europe. Helsinki has the country's main international airport, and an excellent network of smaller airports covers the country. Icebreakers keep the main harbours open through the winter. The Saimaa Canal allows access from the Baltic to the east Finnish lakes and the inland waterways and lakes are served by ferries. The merchant fleet consists mainly of luxury ferries, containers and bulk cargo carriers.

France

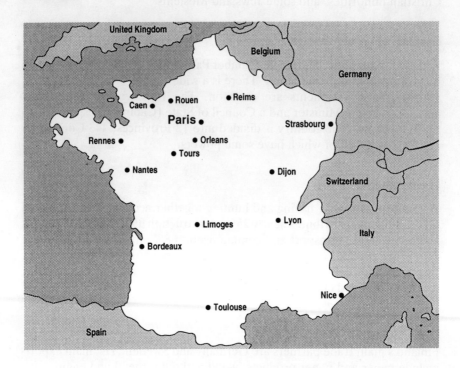

Geography

France is the largest country in Western Europe. It offers a wide variety of scenery, from the Alps and Pyrenees to the river valleys of the Loire, Rhone and Dordogne and the flatter countryside of Normandy. France covers an area of 570,000 square kilometres (210,000 square miles) and the coastline extends to 3,428 kilometres (2,130 miles), including Corsica (644 kilometres or 400 miles). France has land boundaries with Belgium, Luxembourg, Germany, Switzerland, Italy and Spain. The climate is temperate in the north and Mediterranean in the south. The different altitudes and the size of the country provide significant regional climatic variations.

Population

The population of France is about 57 million, with a density of 104 per square kilometre. The capital is Paris, with a population of over two million. Other major cities include Marseilles, Lyons (Lyon), Lille, Toulouse, Nice, Bordeaux and Nantes. French is the official language. There are some regional dialects and Breton, Basque and Corsican are spoken in the appropriate parts of the country. 90% of the population are Roman Catholic, and the rest Protestant, Jewish and Moslem.

Political system

France is a republic. The French Parliament has two chambers, the directly elected National Assembly and the Senate, whose members are chosen by an electoral college. The Executive is led by an elected President who appoints the Prime Minister and the Council of Ministers which administers the country. There are 22 administrative regions with significant financial and administrative powers.

Industry

Agriculture accounts for less than 4% of GDP. Industry, including power, construction, manufacturing and mining, accounts for 30%, and employs about 20% of the workforce. The largest manufacturing sectors are food and transport equipment, followed by chemicals and metals. Tourism, finance, insurance, business services and property are significant. France is a world leader in computing and telecommunications.

Trade

France's main trading partners are Germany, Italy, the UK, Netherlands and Luxembourg. The main exports include machinery, vehicles, chemicals, arms, agricultural produce and wine. Imports include machinery, transport equipment and mineral fuels.

Transport system

The motorways extend to over 6,000 kilometres (3,725 miles), most of which radiate out of Paris. Tolls are charged for the use of many of these. There are over 28,000 kilometres of main roads and a variety of minor roads. The public transport systems in the towns and cities are excellent. Much of the extensive railway network has been electrified to allow high speed trains to link the country. A high speed link from Paris to the Channel Tunnel has been constructed. There are two international airports at Paris. Some international flights also use Bordeaux, Lille, Lyons (Lyon), Marseilles, Nice and Toulouse. Domestic flights link the regions. There are almost 9,000 kilometres (5,600 miles) of navigable waterways in France. Ferries link France with neighbouring countries.

Germany

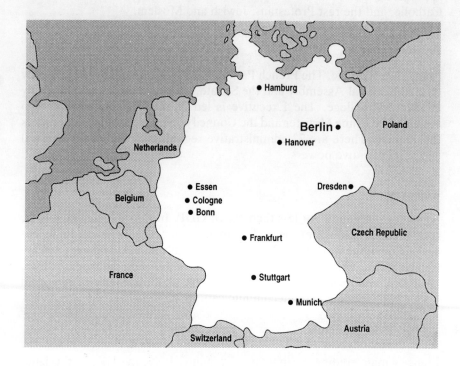

Geography

Germany has a varied geography, ranging from forests and lakes, hills and mountains to the industrial areas of the west. It borders Denmark, Poland, the Czech Republic, Austria, Switzerland, France, Luxembourg, Belgium and the Netherlands. Germany covers an area of 357,000 square kilometres (138,000 square miles) with a coastline of 2,399 kilometres (1,485 miles), including islands. Major rivers include the Rhine, Elbe and Danube. The climate is temperate, giving warm summers and cold winters. Alpine and continental influences are more marked in the south and east of the country respectively.

Population

With a population of 79 million (62 million in the former West Germany and 17 million in the East), it is the most populous state in the European Union and has a population density of 224 people per square kilometre. The capital is Berlin, with a population of 3.4 million but the seat of government is at

Bonn (population 290,000) where the Upper House will remain. The rest, except for eight Federal Ministries, will be transferred to Berlin within the next few years. Other major cities include Munich, Hamburg, Frankfurt, Leipzig and Dresden. The official language is German with some Danish in Schleswig-Holstein. There are some very strong regional dialects. Accurate figures on religion are hard to obtain. In the West, Roman Catholics and Protestants are almost equally divided, and in the East about 35% are Protestant and 7% Catholic. There are also Jewish and Moslem minorities.

System of government

Germany is a federal republic. Parliament is divided into an upper chamber (Bundesrat), which represents the states, and a lower chamber (Bundestag) of popularly elected deputies. The Federal Chancellor is elected by the Bundestag. Each state or Land is organised in the same way, with a parliament and a head of state. The Federal Government has control of defence, foreign affairs and finance. The Länder have their own legislature, government and constitution, and act independently on other matters. Germany was reunited in 1990, and elections were held on 2 December 1990.

Industry

The reunification of Germany has meant that accurate figures are less easily available than they were, but it would appear that agriculture employs about 5% of the working population and industry, including power, manufacturing and construction, just over 40% and accounts for over 35% of GDP. The main manufacturing sectors are chemicals, vehicles, engineering and technology.

Trade

Germany's main trading partners are France, Benelux, Italy, USA and the UK. The main exports are machinery, transport equipment, chemicals and manufactures. Imports include chemical and electrical goods, mining, agricultural and forestry equipment and vehicles.

Transport system

The West is covered by a modern motorway system of more than 10,000 kilometres (6,500 miles). There is an additional 485,000 kilometres (300,000 miles) of road which covers every part of the country. The roads in the East are reasonable, though minor roads may not have good surfaces. They are being improved at the moment, but this process will take time. Public transport is good in all the major towns and cities. The railways in the West of Germany are regular, modern, efficient, with inter-city and local services. In the East, services are less frequent, but a programme of modernisation is taking place. There are a large number of international airports and frequent internal flights linking them. Many rivers have regular boat services, and there are ferries linking German ports to the rest of Europe.

Greece

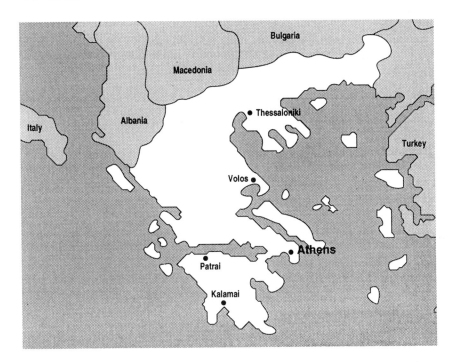

Geography

About one fifth of the land mass comprises of many small islands. Greece covers an area of 132,000 square kilometres (51,000 square miles) of which 29% is arable, 40% meadows and pastures and 20% forest. It has a coastline of 13,700 kilometres (8,500 miles) and borders Albania, Macedonia, Bulgaria and Turkey. The climate is warm Mediterranean with hot summers and mild winters.

Population

Greece has a population of about ten million, at a density of 78 per square kilometre. The capital is Athens with a population of 885,000. Other major cities include Salonika, Piraeus and Patras (Patrai). The official language is Greek, with some Macedonian and Albanian spoken. Most of the population are Greek Orthodox, with Moslem and Roman Catholic minorities.

System of government

Greece is a parliamentary democracy in which the members of Parliament are elected by proportional representation. The Prime Minister is the leader of the largest party in Parliament. The President is elected by Parliament and acts as head of state, though he has no executive power. The country is divided into ten regions, with 51 departments. The local councils have some power.

Industry

Agriculture, including fishing and forestry, is important. Manufacturing includes food products, textiles, metal products, electrical machinery and beverages. Tourism is a major industry. Greece owns the largest shipping fleet in the world.

Trade

Greece's main trading partners are Italy, France and the UK. The main exports are clothing, fruit and vegetables, textiles, wine and tobacco and imports include machinery, transport equipment, food, animals and fuel.

Transport system

Communication is made difficult by a mountainous interior, and so the system is under-developed. The main towns and cities of Greece are served by a reasonable road system, but some of the minor roads are not well-surfaced. Generally speaking, the tourist islands have good main roads, but the minor roads are sometimes narrow and poorly surfaced. A bus network links Athens and many other towns. Athens has trains to many towns at least once a day. There is an international airport at Athens, and at the major tourist islands. There are also internal flights joining the country and its islands. There are ferries between the mainland and the islands, and between many of the islands.

Iceland

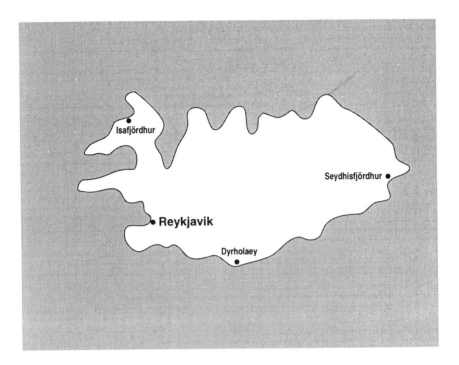

Geography

Iceland is a large island near to the Arctic Circle. It is rugged, beautiful, and largely uninhabited with a number of active volcanoes. Iceland covers an area of 103,000 square kilometres (39,700 square miles) and the coastline extends for 5,000 kilometres (3,100 miles). The climate is moderated by the Gulf Stream, so that summers are relatively mild, and winters cold though with less snow than might be expected.

Population

Iceland has a population of about 250,000 giving a population density of 2.5 per square kilometre. The capital is Reykjavik, with a population of almost 100,000. Other major towns are Kopavogur, Akureyi and Hafnarfjordur. The official language is Icelandic, though English and Danish are widely spoken. Most of the population are Lutheran, with other Protestant minorities.

System of government

Iceland is a republic. The members of the single chamber Parliament (Althing) are elected by proportional representation. The President is elected, and appoints the Prime Minister and the Cabinet.

Industry

The main industries are agriculture, fishing and forestry, which contribute 12% to GDP. Minerals such as aluminium and nitrates are produced. The production of knitwear, blankets and textiles is growing.

Trade

Iceland's main trading partners are Germany, Denmark, Norway and the UK. Fisheries account for almost 80% of exports. Much of the rest is mineral fuel and lubricants. The main imports are machinery and consumer goods.

Transport system

Roads serve all settlements. There are 12,000 kilometres (7,500 miles) of roads, which are often covered in gravel rather than tar. There is no railway system on the island, but a bus service connects the major centres. There are 12 local airports, with domestic services. Ferries serve all local ports in the summer, but poor weather often causes problems in winter.

Ireland

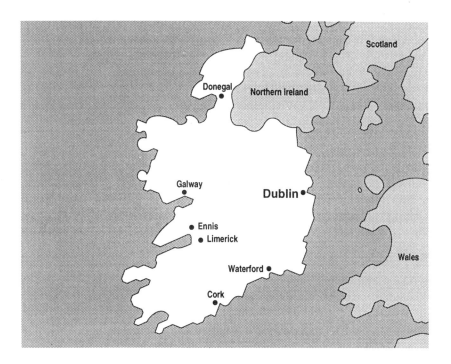

Geography

Ireland is known as "the Emerald Isle" because there is a ring of highlands surrounding peaty lowland areas. It covers an area of 70,000 square kilometres (27,000 square miles) of which 17% is arable, 51% meadows and pastures, 3% forest and 2% inland water. The coastline covers 1,488 kilometres (900 miles). Ireland's only land border is with the UK. The climate is temperate, with warm summers and cool, wet winters.

Population

Ireland's population is almost four million, with a population density of 50 per square mile. The capital is Dublin with a population of almost one million. Other major cities include Cork and Limerick. Gaelic is the official language, but many do not speak it fluently and English is the language most commonly used. 95% are Roman Catholic and most of the remainder are Protestant.

System of government

Ireland is a republic. There are two chambers. The Senate (Seanad Eirann) has elected and appointed members, and only limited powers. The members of the House of Representatives (Dail Eirann) are elected by proportional representation. The President, who is the constitutional Head of State, is elected. The Prime Minister (Toaiseach) is nominated by the House of Representatives and appointed by the President. The country is divided into 26 counties, which have some powers.

Industry

The main industries include agriculture, which employs about 13% of the workforce, and service industries, including finance, transport, communications and commerce. Tourism is also important. International banking is a significant sector and appears to be gaining in importance.

Trade

Ireland's main trading partners are the UK, the USA and Germany. The main exports include machinery, food (especially dairy produce and beef), animals and chemicals. Imports include machinery, food, animals and chemicals.

Transport system

Roads link all of Ireland. There are few motorways but the main roads are being improved as a result of EU grants. Minor roads are not always of good quality. Express trains link the main towns. International flights serve Dublin, Shannon, Cork, Knock and Galway, while smaller airports are used by domestic traffic. There are several ferry services between Irish ports and England and France.

Italy

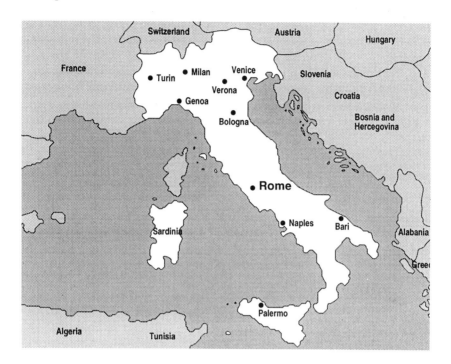

Geography

Italy is a long, mountainous peninsula, and includes the large islands of Sicily and Sardinia. The peninsula is about 1,100 kilometres in length, with a total area of 301,000 square kilometres (116,250 square miles) of which 50% is cultivated, 17% meadow and pasture and 21% forest. The coastline extends to 5,000 kilometres (3,100 miles). Italy borders Slovenia, Austria, Switzerland and France. The climate varies greatly, from temperate in the north, changing to Mediterranean in the south.

Population

The population is 57 million, at a density of 192 per square kilometre. The capital is Rome with a population of four million. Other major cities include Milan, Naples, Turin, Genoa, Bologna, Florence, Catania and Venice. The official language is Italian, with Sardinian, Slovene, French and German spoken in some areas. The people are mostly Roman Catholic.

System of government

Italy is a parliamentary democracy with a Republican Constitution. There are elected upper and lower houses of Parliament with similar legislative functions. The head of state is the President, who is elected by the members of the houses of Parliament and representatives of the regional governments. The President appoints the Prime Minister and, on his recommendation, the other ministers. Since the war, Italy has been governed by a series of short-lived coalitions. The 20 regions have considerable executive power. The Vatican City is a separate sovereign state under the jurisdiction of the Pope.

Industries

Italy possesses limited natural resources. There is some mining, including lead, zinc and magnesium, but only one coal mine, at Sulcis in Sardinia. Natural gas is produced in the Adriatic and oil south of Sicily. Italy is self sufficient in agriculture, and is Europe's largest grower of fruit and vegetables. This sector employs about 9% of Italy's workforce, of whom about two-thirds are self employed, but contributes only about 3.5% of GDP. Manufacturing includes machinery and transport equipment, electrical goods, textiles, clothing and chemicals. Tourism is a significant industry.

Trade

Italy suffers from trade deficits, but this is compensated by inflows of foreign capital and remittances from Italians working abroad. The main trading partners are Germany and France, Latin America and the USA. The main exports include vehicles and transport equipment, industrial machinery, chemicals and clothes. Imports include oil and raw materials.

Transport system

Italy has an extensive network of motorways. Tolls are levied on many of these. Other roads, though adequate, are much slower. Rail links are good between the main towns, with high speed trains between Milan and Rome. Fares are low in comparison with those in the UK. There are airports in Rome, Milan, Pisa (for Florence), Turin, Venice, Naples and Genoa providing frequent international and internal flights. Ferry services operate between the mainland and offshore islands as well as between the Italian ports and other Mediterranean destinations.

Liechtenstein

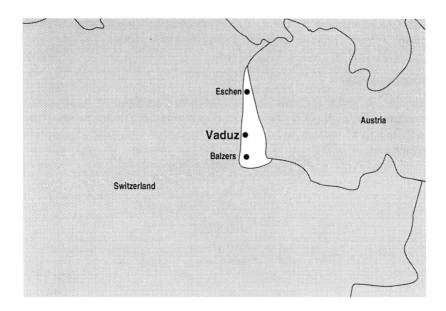

Geography

Liechtenstein is small and landlocked. It covers an area of 160 square kilometres (62 square miles) and borders Austria and Switzerland. The climate is moderate continental, with warm, wet summers and coldish winters.

Population

The population is about 30,000 giving a density of 184 per square kilometre. The capital is Vaduz with a population of almost 5,000. The official language is German. The religion is mainly Roman Catholic with some Protestants.

System of government

Liechtenstein is an hereditary principality. The members of Parliament (Landtag) are elected by proportional representation, and Parliament elects the government. The sovereign is head of state but has no executive powers.

Industry

Industry consists of metals, machine tools and precision instruments. Banking is a major service industry.

Trade

The main trading partner is Switzerland. The main exports are artificial teeth and dental products, metal, machinery and precision instruments and furniture. Imports include machinery and consumer goods.

Transport system

The roads are good, and are similar in standard to those of Austria and Switzerland. Buses link the centres of population. The main railway line from Zurich to Vienna passes through Liechtenstein. The nearest airport is at Zurich.

Luxembourg

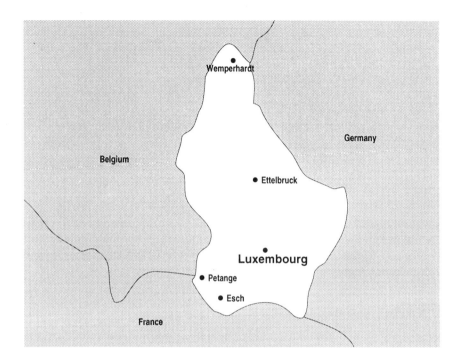

Geography

Luxembourg is a small, landlocked country, made up of hills, forests and wooded farmland. It borders on France, Belgium and Germany and covers an area of 2,590 square kilometres (1,000 square miles). The climate is temperate, being warm in summer, with snow in winter.

Population

The population is 0.37 million, at a density of 151 per square kilometre. The capital is Luxembourg, with a population of 75,000. Other towns include Esch/Alzette and Differdange. The official language is a German-Moselle-Frankish dialect, but the commercial language is German, and French is also used. Most of the population is Roman Catholic, with Protestant and Jewish minorities.

System of government

Luxembourg is a constitutional monarchy. The single chamber Parliament, the Chamber of Deputies, is elected by proportional representation. The ruler, the Grand Duke, appoints the Prime Minister, who leads the Council of Ministers, which is responsible to the Chamber of Deputies. The country is divided into Cantons, or administrative regions.

Industry

Agriculture is of little importance. Iron and steel, chemicals, rubber and plastic, machinery and printing are the main industries. There is a significant financial services sector.

Trade

Luxembourg's main trading partners are Belgium, Germany and France. The main exports are basic metals and manufactures, plastics, rubber and machinery. Imports include mineral products, basic manufactured goods, transport machinery and chemicals.

Transport system

The road system is excellent, and cross-country buses operate between the towns. The rail system is fully integrated with the bus network to provide a very efficient service. There is a modern international airport.

Netherlands

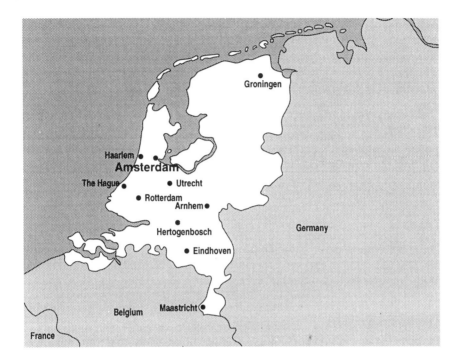

Geography

Large areas of the Netherlands have been reclaimed from the sea, and 20% of the country is below sea level. The area is flat, and has many rivers and canals. The Netherlands borders on Belgium and Germany. It covers an area of 34,000 square kilometres (13,100 square miles) of which 70% is cultivated, 8% forest and 8% inland water. The coastline extends over 451 kilometres (280 miles). The climate is temperate with warm summers and cold winters.

Population

The population is just over 15 million, with a density of 447 per square kilometre, which is the highest in Europe. The capital is Amsterdam (population 715,000), but The Hague (445,000) is the seat of government. Other major cities include Rotterdam, Utrecht, Eindhoven, Haarlem and Groningen. The official language is Dutch, though German, French and English are widely spoken. 30% of the population is Protestant, 38% Roman Catholic and 26% are unaffiliated.

Seat of government

The Netherlands is a constitutional monarchy. The country is divided into 12 Provinces, all of which have elected councils. The Provincial Councils elect the members of the First Chamber. The Second Chamber is directly elected by proportional representation. The Prime Minister is appointed by the Monarch, who then advises on the appointment of the rest of the Council of Ministers. Each Province has a Governor.

Industry

The Netherlands is one of the world's largest exporters of farm produce. Industry is well developed in the areas of heavy engineering, petrochemicals, pharmaceutical products, plastics and synthetic fibres.

Trade

The Netherlands' main trading partners are Germany, Belgium, France and the UK. The main exports are machinery and transport equipment and food. Imports include mineral fuels.

Transport system

There is an excellent road system, and an extensive regional bus network. The rail network is extensive, and the trains are punctual and cheap, with very regular inter-city and regional services. The main international airport is at Amsterdam, but some international fights operate from Rotterdam, Eindhoven and Maastricht. There are also internal flights. Rotterdam is the largest port in Europe. There are ferry services joining the islands and connecting the Netherlands to neighbouring countries.

Norway

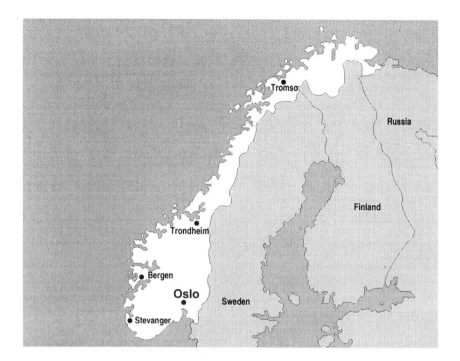

Geography

One of the main features of Norway is the large number of fjords, many of which are between 80–160 kilometres (50–100 miles) long. Norway covers an area of 325,00 square kilometres (125,000 miles) excluding Svalbard (62,000 square kilometres or 24,000 square miles) and Jan Mayen (373 square kilometres or 144 square miles) and the islands 2,400 kilometres (1,500 miles). It borders Finland, Sweden and Russia. Mainland Norway has a coastline of 3,400 kilometres (2,215 miles). The climate varies, being warmer on the coast and in the south, and colder inland and in the north. The northern part of the country is inside the Arctic Circle, but due to the influence of the Gulf Stream, ports are ice-free in winter.

Population

Norway has a population of 4.25 million, giving a density of 13 per square kilometre. The capital is Oslo, with a population of 467,000. Other major cities include Bergen, Trondheim and Stavanger. The official language is

Norwegian with Lapp spoken in the north. 92% of the population are Evangelical Lutherans, with other Christian minorities.

System of government

Norway is a constitutional monarchy. The Parliament (Storting) is elected by proportional representation. It is divided into an upper house (Lagting) and a lower house (Odelsting). The Monarch appoints the Council of Ministers on the recommendation of the Storting, and it is led by a Prime Minister. The country is divided into counties, communes and towns.

Industry

Agriculture, forestry and fishing are significant. Fish farming is growing. Hydro-electrical power has reduced costs for industry, and Norway has become a major oil exporter.

Trade

Norway's main partners are Sweden, Germany, the UK, the USA and Japan. The main exports are petroleum and natural gas. Imports include machinery and transport equipment.

Transport system

Due to the nature of the terrain, communications are difficult in Norway. The quality of the roads varies, especially in the north, where poor weather conditions can make driving very difficult. The rail network links the main cities. There are international airports at Oslo, Stavanger and Bergen, and a comprehensive network of domestic services joins the towns and cities. All coastal towns are served by ferries.

Portugal

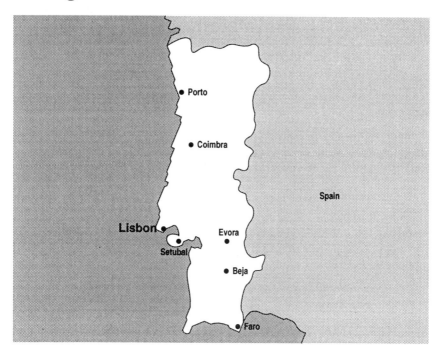

Geography

Portugal covers an area of 92,300 square kilometres (35,675 square miles) including Madeira and the Azores, of which 48% is arable, 6% meadow and pasture and 31% forest. Mainland Portugal has a coastline of 860 kilometres (535 miles), Madeira 225 kilometres (140 miles) and the Azores 708 kilometres (440 miles). The only land border is with Spain. The climate varies according to region. The north west has short summers and mild winters, the north east warmer summers with longer winters, and the south has warm, dry summers.

Population

Portugal has a population of about ten million, at a density of 106 per square kilometre. The capital is Lisbon, with a population of 808,000. The other major city is Oporto (Porto). The official language is Portuguese. The population is almost exclusively Roman Catholic.

System of government

Portugal is a republic. The Assembly of the Republic is directly elected. The Head of State is the President, who is elected. The President appoints the Prime Minister, and then recommends the other members of the Council of Ministers. Portugal is divided into Districts. Madeira and the Azores are part of the Republic, but have autonomous governments.

Industry

Agriculture, including fishing, forestry and wine, employs nearly 25% of the working population. Textiles and clothing manufacture are important and there is a significant footwear industry. Tourism is an important industry.

Trade

Portugal's main trading partners are Spain, Germany, France and the UK. The main exports are clothing and footwear, paper, ceramics and electrical appliances. Petroleum is the main import.

Transport system

All towns and villages can be reached by road, and some motorways exist. They are subject to a toll. There is a rail service to most towns. There are international airports at Lisbon, Faro and Oporto (Porto) and some internal flights. There are a number of ports, and some ferry services.

Spain

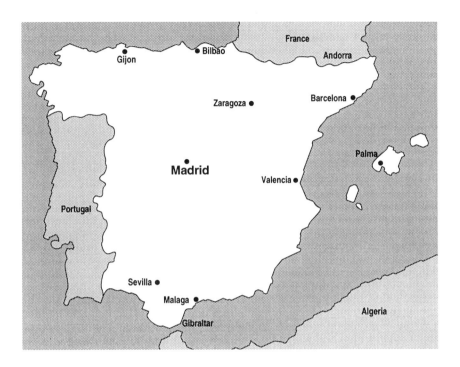

Geography

Spain is the second largest country in Western Europe, covering an area of 505,000 square kilometres (195,000 square miles) including the Canaries (7,500 square kilometres or 2,900 square miles) and the Balearics (5,025 square kilometres or 1,940 square miles) of which 41% is arable, 27% meadow and pasture, and 22% forest. The coastline covers 5,000 kilometres (3,085 miles), including the Canaries (1,160 kilometres or 720 miles), and the Balearies (677 kilometres or 420 miles). Spain has land borders with France and Portugal. The climate is Mediterranean with hot summers and cold winters. There are continental influences in the interior.

Population

Spain has a population of 39 million at a density of 77 per square kilometre. The capital is Madrid with a population of 3 million. Other major cities include Barcelona, Valencia and Seville (Sevilla). Spanish is the official language, with Catalan in the North East, Galician in the North West and

Basque in the North. The population is mainly Roman Catholic with some Moslems and a few Protestants and Jews.

System of government

The Parliament (Cortes) has two houses. The Congress of Deputies is elected by proportional representation and the Senate is directly elected. The King is head of state. He appoints the President, and on his recommendation the other members of the Council of Ministers. Spain is divided into 17 regions, with an elected Council and a Governor. There is considerable regional self-government.

Industry

Agriculture and fishing contributes 4% of GDP. The manufacturing of motor cars, footwear and textiles, chemicals and steel is significant. The tourist industry is a vital part of the Spanish economy.

Trade

Spain's main trading partners are France and Germany. The main exports are cars, machinery, iron and steel goods and agricultural produce. Imports include mineral fuels, petroleum and chemical products, machinery, electrical equipment and vehicles.

Transport system

There are more than 150,000 kilometres (95,000 miles) of road. The motorways are well maintained, and a toll charge is usually made. The major roads are good, but the minor roads are of varied quality. The rail network joins the major towns and cities. There are international airports at Alicante, Barcelona, Bilboa, Madrid, Malaga, Santiago de Compostela, Seville (Sevilla) and Valencia. Scheduled internal flights connect all the main towns and islands. There are regular ferries to north Africa and to the Spanish islands.

Sweden

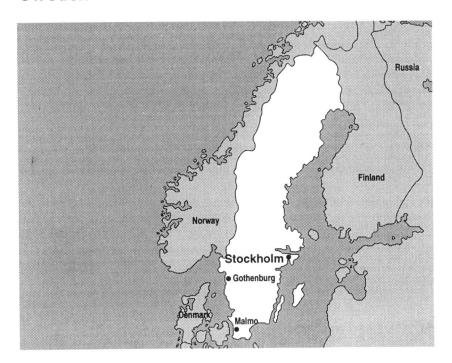

Geography

About half of the country is covered in forest, and there are thousands of lakes in the southern central area. Sweden covers an area of 441,000 square kilometres (170,250 square miles) of which 8% is cultivated, 1% meadows and pastures and 55% forest. The coastline covers 3,200 kilometres (2,000 miles). Sweden has land borders with Norway and Finland. Despite its northerly position, Sweden has a relatively mild climate, with warm summers and cold winters. Temperatures vary with latitude, being colder and drier in the north and milder and wetter in the south west.

Population

Sweden has a population of 8.7 million at a density of 19 per square kilometre. The capital is Stockholm with a population of 685,000. Other major cities include Gothenburg and Malmö. The official language is Swedish, with Lapp and Finnish spoken by minorities. Most of the population are Lutheran Protestant, with other Protestant minorities.

System of government

Sweden is a constitutional monarchy. It has a single chamber Parliament, the Riksdag, whose members are elected directly by proportional representation. The Prime Minister and Cabinet are drawn from the largest party or coalition of parties. The King is head of state but has limited powers. Local government is administered through about 280 municipalities, which have significant power, including town planning, social welfare, education, child care, recreation and culture.

Industry

Agriculture contributes 2%, construction 9.5%, wholesaling, retailing and restaurants 13%, and mining and manufacture 19%, transport, communications, banking, insurance, property management and education 22%, and central and local government 22% of GDP. Private companies account for 85% of industrial employment, government 10% and co-operatives 5%. The service sector has grown at the expense of manufacturing, and has reached a 70–30 split. Mining and manufacturing employ one fifth of the work force.

Trade

Sweden's main trading partners are Germany, the UK, Norway and the USA. The main exports are machinery and transport equipment, wood and wood products. Imports include machinery and transport equipment, mineral fuels and foodstuffs.

Transport system

The road quality is good. Roads carry 90% of passengers and 60% of freight. Traffic is concentrated in southern Sweden. Swedish Railways operate a network, mostly electrified, of about 12,000 kilometres, which is the largest per capita in Europe. Fares are high, but the system is efficient. The major domestic airline is Scandinavian Airlines System (SAS), which is jointly owned by Danish, Norwegian and Swedish groups. There are international airports at Stockholm, Gothenburg and Malmö, and domestic flights serve about 40 Swedish towns and cities. Most Swedish imports arrive by sea, and there are car ferries.

Switzerland

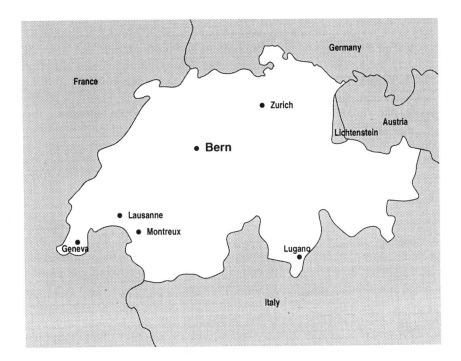

Geography

Switzerland is landlocked and has the highest mountains in Europe as well as waterfalls and lakes. It has borders with Austria, Liechtenstein, France, Germany and Italy. It covers an area of 41,250 square kilometres (16,000 square miles) including 10% arable, 43% meadows and pastures, 24% forest and 3% inland water. The climate is moderate continental but varies considerably with topography.

Population

Switzerland has a population of 6.8 million of which 16% are foreign nationals. It has a density of 166 per square kilometre. The capital is Berne (Bern) with a population of 135,000. Other major cities include Zurich, Basle, Geneva and Lausanne. There are three official languages – German (with various dialects), which is spoken by 65%, French spoken by 18%, and Italian by 10%. The remainder use Romansch and other languages. The population is almost evenly divided between Roman Catholic and Protestant.

System of government

Switzerland is a confederation. It is divided into 26 cantons and half cantons, each with elected assemblies, and over 3,000 communes. The Federal Assembly or Parliament has two chambers: the Council of States with elected members representing the cantons and the National Council elected directly by proportional representation. The Federal Council has seven members including the President who is elected, according to a special political and linguistic formula, by the Federal Assembly. It holds executive power. The President acts as head of state for one year. The members of the federal council hold the Presidency in rotation. The Federal Government deals with defence and foreign and economic policy while the cantons have considerable autonomy in other areas of government.

Industry

Water is the only significant natural resource and is important for electricity generation, though nuclear power is also used. Industries include precision manufacturing, such as clock and watch making, machine tools, printing and photographic equipment and chemicals. Services including the financial sector and tourism are vital to the economy.

Trade

Switzerland's main trading partners are Germany, France, Italy and the UK. The main exports include electrical and mechanical engineering, machinery, metal and chemical products, precision instruments, textiles and clothing. Imports include energy, machinery, metal products, motor vehicles and chemicals. Switzerland is a founder member of EFTA and in May 1992 it applied to join the European Union, but in December 1992 the people voted against joining the European Economic Area, so entry is likely to be delayed.

Transport system

The motorways and main roads are well engineered and surfaced, but snow and ice can cause serious problems in winter. There is also a dense network of minor roads in the lowland areas. There are frequent rail services between cities, together with comprehensive connecting services. There are excellent airports at Zurich, Geneva and Basle-Mulhouse with frequent international and domestic flights. Zurich and Geneva have mainline railway stations within the air terminal, linking to the towns and cities. There are smaller airports at Berne (Bern) and Lugano.

The United Kingdom

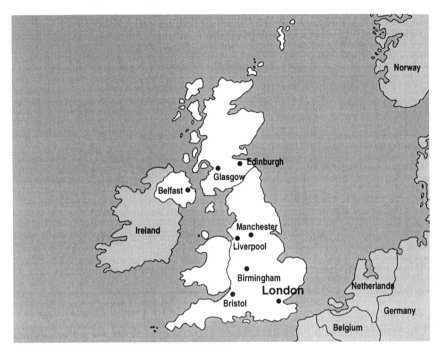

Geography

The UK covers an area of 244,000 square kilometres (152,500 square miles) of which 30% is arable, 50% meadow and pasture, 7% forest and 1% inland water. The coastline covers 12,400 kilometres (7,725 miles). The climate is temperate.

Population

The UK population is 57.5 million of which 81% is English, 9% Scottish, 5% Welsh, 3% Irish and 2% other ethnic immigrants. The population density is 238 per square kilometre. The capital is London with a population of 6.8 million. Other major cities include Birmingham, Glasgow, Leeds, Liverpool, Manchester and Sheffield. The official language is English, with Welsh and Scots Gaelic spoken. The religion is mainly Church of England, with other Protestants and Roman Catholics, and sizeable Moslem, Hindu and Jewish minorities.

System of government

The UK is a constitutional monarchy. The Monarch is head of state. There are two assemblies. The lower house, the House of Commons, has direct election. The upper house, the House of Lords, consists of hereditary or life peers or peeresses. The Prime Minister appoints the cabinet and is responsible to the House of Commons.

Industry

Agriculture and fishing are important, but only employ 3% of the population. Industries include petrochemicals, heavy engineering, electronics and textiles. Tourism and the financial sector are vital parts of the economy.

Trade

The UK's main trading partners are the members of the European Union and the USA. The main exports are machinery and transport equipment and chemicals. Imports include vehicles, office equipment, paper, food, manufactured goods and textiles.

Transport system

There is a good motorway system which, together with the other main roads, link the main towns and cities. The minor roads are not always so modern. A coach system links the cities. The rail network provides fast services to London, and there are links to the other towns. However, rural areas are not always accessible by rail. The Channel Tunnel has created a direct rail link with France. Most large cities have international airports, and there are regular domestic flights. A variety of ports offer ferry links to Europe and to Ireland.

Activity

- Students, either working on their own or in groups, should select a country which is not included in this book.
- The students should then decide on the information that would be required in order to include this country in Chapter 1.
- The students should draw a map of the country, and indicate the main cities and towns.
- They should then decide what sources they should consult in order to compile the information.
- Armed with these sources, the students should be given sufficient time to gain the required information.
- Once the information has been gathered and put into a presentable format, the whole cohort should come together, and in turns, offer the material to their contemporaries. They should indicate their sources, and explain any difficulties that they have encountered.
- Thus, details on several additional countries should have been added, and these can be developed in later activities.
- Moreover, this could be the basis for an assessment, as it offers the students an opportunity to develop research skills within a confined framework.

Chapter Two

The Post-War European Environment

Aims of this chapter

□ To provide a broad outline of the post-war situation in Western Europe in order to highlight key problem areas

□ To give the reader a brief insight into economic recovery

□ To analyse the role of the United States in that recovery

□ To show how the European Union has evolved from relatively modest beginnings based on differing perceptions

□ To highlight institutional development (as this is crucial to understanding Chapter Three)

□ To give a preliminary outline of the UK's attitude (which is developed further in Chapter Eight)

□ To illustrate the difficulties which arose during the 1970s and 1980s and the controversies engendered by the Delors proposals and the Maastricht Treaty

□ To outline key issues since the ratification of the Maastricht Treaty

Many excellent works on European history already exist. This chapter therefore does not seek to compete with these or to offer a reinterpretation of what other authors have written. Instead, it is designed to give the reader a brief overview of certain key developments which are of particular relevance in the context of this volume. If more detailed information is required, the reader should consult a more specialised work. Within this chapter, the emphasis has been deliberately placed on the emergence and development of integrative structures in Western Europe.

European unity is generally associated with the post-war era – specifically with the emergence of pan-European institutions such as the European Union.

However, history shows that the idea is much older, though exactly how old is not wholly clear.

It might be argued that the Roman conquest of much of Europe imposed a unifying culture and set of values. In medieval times some scholars saw the Universal (Roman Catholic) Church as the unifying factor and all Christian states were therefore perceived as belonging to a vast family under the wing of that Church.

In more recent times both Napoleon and Hitler sought to impose unity by the use of military force. Both failed and disastrous wars were the result. Following the Napoleonic Wars, the Congress of Vienna attempted to construct a stable political regime for Europe based on the concept of the balance of power on the continent. This eventually failed – not least because it rested on the assumption that the relative strengths of the major powers would remain unchanged.

The cessation of hostilities on the European continent in May 1945 was greeted with a mixture of relief and euphoria – at least among those who had emerged victorious. Once the actual fighting was over, however, the wartime alliance which had united the United States, the UK and the Soviet Union soon collapsed. The early post-war years were thus marked by tension and anxiety, by mutual recrimination and non-comprehension. The Cold War and the division of Europe into two distinct camps were the direct results of this breakdown.

One of the most serious issues concerned the future of Germany, on which no concrete agreement had been reached before hostilities ended. Indeed it was the German question which provoked the split between East and West which physically and psychologically scarred the continent until the very end of the 1980s.

Nearly six years of warfare had taken their toll – both in terms of physical damage and of lives lost. Moreover, there was an economic cost in terms of the productive capacity which had been lost, which affected all belligerent with the exception of the United States. In the case of the UK, this was compounded by the fact that the country had exhausted its reserves of gold and convertible currency in order to finance the war effort. Britain now found itself heavily indebted to its principal ally, the United States, as well as to many Commonwealth countries for goods supplied during wartime.

If we leave military considerations (such as the perceived threat posed by the Soviet Union) aside, the problems confronting post-war Europe might be summarised as follows:

- physical regeneration (in other words the reconstruction of the infra-structure, the industrial and commercial base and of communications);
- economic regeneration (in other words the financing of recovery, especially in view of Britain's perilous financial situation) and the need to make European business competitive;
- the consequences of division (which became increasingly apparent with the growing deterioration of inter-Allied relations);

- the status of Germany.

Many believed that given the failure of the existing political system (based on the concept of the nation-state), only pan-European organisations would reshape Europe to address issues such as those listed above and also remove potential sources of conflict. Nevertheless, it was clear that in the shorter term European states could make only a limited contribution to the continent's recovery.

European recovery

Reconstruction was clearly dependent on the availability of funding. Despite long-standing British expertise in the provision of finance, it was the United States which made the major contribution to economic recovery in the form of Marshall Aid. In any event few, if any, of the European states involved in World War II were in any position to make a major contribution to recovery in the short term. The United States, on the other hand, had significant reserves of capital together with spare capacity and goods to sell. At least superficially, Marshall Aid can be viewed as an exercise in philanthropy. Secretary of State George C. Marshall himself announced that the aid programme would be used to eradicate "hunger, poverty, desperation and chaos". However, in the same speech Marshall let it be known that there was also a political agenda. According to Marshall, the purpose was to promote "free institutions". In other words, President Truman and his advisers fully understood that while states such as Poland and the Soviet Union plainly needed the money as much as any in the West, the absence of "free institutions" meant that they would be excluded from American generosity. Thus, while Marshall Aid undoubtedly made an invaluable contribution to the revival of economic activity in the West, we should not forget that it was largely driven by political (and military) concerns. It could also be argued that the programme created a substantial business opportunity for the United States. Moreover, it also eased the restructuring of the US economy from a wartime to a peacetime footing by making clever use of spare capacity and thus lessening the danger of massive unemployment.

The perceived military threat had caused Western European countries to develop mechanisms for co-ordinating their defence efforts in the early post-war years. Parallel to these, attempts were made to develop a stable political and economic system appropriate to post-war conditions. While this was to a large extent the product of the post-war situation, it also seems true that events between the wars were a significant factor. Perhaps one of the bitterest lessons of the 1930s was that individual states acting independently of each other had been able to do little to mitigate the effects of the Great Depression; indeed it may well be true that the policy of putting national priorities first actually prolonged the recession. By the same token, it is arguable that the experience of the inter-war years demonstrated the need for a co-operation regime in Europe. While this was plainly important enough in itself, the existence of such a regime would have made a repeat of the Second World War less likely.

The rise of Nazism in Germany undoubtedly owed much to the economic conditions prevailing at the time – massive unemployment and hyper-inflation – against which the country appeared powerless. At the same time, Germany was relatively isolated politically. Once in power, Hitler had been able to offer a solution to the country's economic ills, while at the same time fanning the flames of resentment at Germany's isolation into the most obscene excesses of narrow, aggressive, nationalism, the main consequence of which was the Second World War. Had Germany been in the European mainstream, so to speak, this would not have been achieved so easily.

A new political and economic order in Europe would therefore have to ensure that a revived Germany would be in no position to de-stabilise the rest of the continent. In this respect relations between France and Germany were seen to be paramount, not least given three German invasions of France between 1870 and 1940. Rivalry between the two might have threatened to de-stabilise the continent once again. If the potential for rivalry was removed, then this threat would at least be diminished. It therefore made sense to promote *rapprochement*. In any event, it seems highly unlikely that other European states, such as Belgium, would have been comfortable with the prospect of a revived (West) Germany isolated from the rest of Western Europe.

Deteriorating East-West relations and the advent of the Cold War also played a part in determining the future of West Germany. From a Western standpoint, any military arrangements necessary to counter the apparent threat depended heavily on West German participation. However, this in turn depended on the extent to which the West was prepared to trust the FRG (future reunified Germany). If the FRG was to be integrated militarily into the West, it also made much sense to ensure that it was part of integrative Western European economic and political structures. Once firmly anchored in the West, the FRG, would be in no position to de-stabilise the rest of the European continent. Moreover, it would have a clear stake in Europe's future.

The First Step

Since the late 1940s, much progress has been made towards the economic and political integration of Western Europe. It is therefore worth recalling that the first step in the process was a modest one indeed. The Benelux Customs Union was formed in 1947 by Belgium, the Netherlands and Luxembourg. These three small countries agreed to the removal of customs tariffs on goods moving within the union. An economic union was established in October 1947 and the Customs Union came into effect on 1 January 1948.

The logic of this step is easy enough to identify. The three are in close proximity to each other, sandwiched between two much larger states, France and Germany. Their economies were to some extent interlinked. Moreover, all three had been neutral prior to 1940 but had seen their neutrality violated. It could therefore be said that the three (whom we tend to think of today as a natural partnership) had shared responsibilities and interests together with shared historical experience – albeit unpleasant.

The establishment of the Benelux Customs Union represents one trend in the history of post-war European integration – the promotion of the free movement of goods. While the Customs Union may have been over-shadowed by subsequent developments, it was a highly significant – if small – step. However, sector agreements had an equally important role to play, as the example of the European Coal and Steel Community shows. The establishment of the European Economic Community can be seen as the point where the two trends converge.

The European Coal and Steel Community (ECSC)

The origins of the ECSC owe much to the concerns mentioned above. The Treaty of Paris, signed on 18 April 1951, removed the coal and steel industries from domestic control (whether public or private) and placed them under a supra-national authority. Six countries – France, Belgium, the Netherlands, Luxembourg, Italy and West Germany – agreed to this step. The UK had been invited to participate but had declined to do so. Even today, it remains unclear whether this was motivated by lack of confidence in the viability of the proposal, by domestic priorities (these industries having been nationalised by the Attlee government) or by the prospect of French opposition.

By agreeing to joint administration of key industries, the six had removed a potential source of conflict. The agreement also went some way to addressing the problem of Franco-German relations. As a result of the Treaty, it was now possible to restore West Germany's heavy industrial base but without allowing it to be used for purely national military purposes and thus posing a threat to the country's neighbours, such as France and the Benelux countries. At the same time, the Treaty placed France and West Germany, the two largest states in continental Western Europe, in the same camp with shared responsibilities. It also seems likely that the restoration of the Saar (a key industrial area then under French administration) to West Germany was made simpler through the Treaty.

The existence of the ECSC is due largely to the efforts of two far-sighted Frenchmen – Jean Monnet and Robert Schuman. According to Schuman the ECSC was to be the first in a series of European Communities, the object of which was ". . . to make war not merely unthinkable but materially impossible. . . ". The larger purpose was not merely to administer strategically important industries but to pave the way for an integrated European system of military security. This, however, has yet to be achieved.

More specifically, the ECSC was intended to regulate the market in the coal and steel industries by agreeing on prices, production and investment policy. Broadly speaking, the object was to ensure regular availability of these key products at stable prices, to promote modernisation and expansion. In other words, it was more than a free trade area for a limited range of products.

Moreover, the ECSC encompassed a social dimension in its aim to provide better working and living conditions for those employed in the coal and steel industries. ECSC policies also addressed such issues as redundancies and the need for retraining.

What was distinctive about the ECSC, however, concerns its structure rather than its ambitious objectives and policies. In all, four main institutions were established as a result of the Treaty. These were:

- the High Authority
- the Council of Ministers
- the Common Assembly
- the Court of Justice.

According to Article 8 of the Treaty of Paris, the task of the High Authority was to ". . . ensure that the objectives set out in (the) Treaty are attained in accordance with the provisions thereof . . .". The Authority's function was thus largely administrative, though it did also have considerable autonomy in decision-making – certainly more than the European Commission enjoys today. On paper, the High Authority was the most powerful of the new institutions, though it has been criticised for its failure to secure implementation of truly pan-European policies.

The Council of Ministers was, as its title suggests, composed of ministers from member countries. While the Council had a degree of control over some High Authority decisions, its main function was to co-ordinate actions taken by the High Authority with the policies followed by member governments. It owed its existence to concerns expressed by the smaller member states that an institution was needed to balance the power wielded by the High Authority. In this way the interests of the nation-states, the traditional building blocks of the European political system, were represented.

If the European Commission is palpably less powerful than its predecessor, the High Authority, the reverse is true of the Council of Ministers, which is now by some way the most influential of the institutions of the European Union. Nevertheless, the existence of these two symbolised the tension which still exists today between national and European priorities.

The purpose of the Common Assembly was to give a veneer of democracy and accountability to the decision-making process. However, the Assembly's role was largely advisory, though it did have the power to pass a motion of censure on the High Authority. Its members were chosen by national parliaments rather than elected directly, as members of the European Parliament are today.

The Court of Justice was established under the Treaty in order to settle disputes:

- between member states;
- between institutions, and
- between institutions and states.

Perhaps most significantly, the composition of these four institutions was truly multinational with members drawn from all participating states, a practice still followed by the European Union today. At the very least, the ECSC marks a turning point. If nothing else, it established the principle that European and national standpoints existed and that these could be reconciled. How effective the ECSC actually was, is open to debate. On the one hand it was successful in abolishing customs tariffs and quotas for coal and steel, in promoting international co-operation and in facilitating the restructuring of those industries. It would appear that its members achieved notable rates of economic growth in the early years – certainly much higher than those attained by the UK. The Coal and Steel Community also appears to have made a major contribution to the revival of trade within Europe.

However, it could also be said that for the most part the growth rates mentioned above were achieved starting from a relatively low base and that they owed as much to the general post-war recovery as they did to the ECSC. Moreover, it appears that in at least one vital respect the ECSC failed to achieve the objective which it had set itself. By the end of the 1950s a coal crisis had become apparent. A combination of cheap oil imports together with a significant fall in energy consumption meant that coal production had to be reduced. Instead of following the High Authority's pan-European plan, member states chose to respond to domestic priorities. In the event, the High Authority proved unable to enforce its policy and this remains a weakness of the EU today. Within the European Union a free market for coal and steel can still hardly be said to exist.

The European Economic Community

Whatever its weaknesses, the ECSC demonstrated that economic integration could work and it may have suggested that political integration might also be achieved. In June 1955 the Foreign Ministers of the six ECSC countries met in Messina to consider the way forward. In the Messina Declaration, they agreed to work towards a common market and the harmonisation of social policies with a view to ultimately creating a united Europe.

Under the chairmanship of Paul-Henri Spaak, the Belgian Foreign Minister, negotiations began. Britain accepted an invitation to take part but later withdrew. In general terms, the British withdrawal was motivated by the realisation that the Messina Declaration and the substance of the subsequent negotiations went far beyond an earlier British proposal for a loosely structured free trade area with no administrative institutions or common policies. The negotiations, though protracted, eventually resulted in the Treaties of Rome signed on 25 March 1957. These led to the creation of the European Economic Community (EEC) and the European Atomic Energy Authority (EURATOM). At the time, many felt that the second of these would be the more dynamic and successful. However, experience has shown that national governments have been somewhat reluctant to co-operate in the area of nuclear technology.

As a result there were now three Communities in existence with separate structures, though with some shared institutions, such as the Common Assembly. The EEC aimed to create a common market for *all* goods instead of merely coal and steel. The Treaty contained proposals for a common external tariff and for the removal of all internal tariff barriers. It also proposed a common policy on agriculture with the aims of guaranteeing food supplies and supporting farm incomes. The Customs Union was scheduled for completion in 1969, though in fact this was achieved in July 1968, at which point the common external tariff came into operation.

However, the EEC Treaty was much more than an agreement to establish a common market. In addition to detailed proposals governing internal and external trade, it also contained proposals (many of them vague) covering agriculture, competition, gender equality and education. Perhaps most importantly of all, there was a commitment to a social dimension. The preamble to the EEC Treaty states that the aim is ". . . to lay the foundation of an ever closer union among the peoples of Europe . . . to ensure economic and social progress by common action to eliminate the barriers which divide Europe . . . ". The goal might therefore be defined as the attainment of political as well as economic union.

The Merger Treaty of 1967 established a set of common institutions to control all three Communities. While all three continued to exist and to function, a common administrative structure was created. The European Commission, for example, replaced the High Authority of the ECSC, though with rather less power than the latter had enjoyed. The new structure became known as the European Communities or more commonly European Community.

The expanded Community

Critics of the European Union often regard the period from the late 1960 until the mid-1980s as one of stagnation. It is not difficult to support this view. It might appear as if relatively little was achieved during this time. Little progress was made towards some of the Treaty's wider aims, such as a common foreign policy. In contrast, the problems of the Common Agricultural Policy (such as over-production) and those generated by the oil crisis in the mid-1970s seemed all too apparent. Another issue which attracted much attention – especially during the early 1980s – was that of the Community's finances. It appeared that the sheer cost of administering the EC was in danger of outstripping the financial resources at its disposal. For this reason alone, reform was necessary.

For the UK, the size of its contribution was of vital importance. Although the Wilson Government had renegotiated terms of entry in the mid-1970s, many still felt that the overall British contribution was unacceptably high since the agreement had not delivered any significant improvement. The issue came to a head at the Dublin European Council in 1979 when Prime Minister Thatcher insisted on a refund ("Thatcher's billion") leading to acrimonious exchanges. It took until 1984 to reach a compromise agreement largely at the instigation of President Mitterrand. Even so, the Fontainebleau compromise fell short of what many in the UK had hoped for or believed to be just. Moreover, with increases agreed on farm support, France and Germany appeared to have gained at least as much as the UK.

It would be inaccurate to assume that the EC was hamstrung during this period. For one thing, membership had grown to 12 by 1986. After two false starts during the 1960s, the UK acceded on 1 January 1973 along with Ireland and Denmark. Greece became a member in 1981 and Portugal and Spain in 1986. The need to accommodate so many new members in such a short space of time would in itself explain the apparent lack of progress. In any event, some positive developments should also be recorded here – such as the creation of the Regional Development Fund in the mid-1970s and the establishment of European Monetary system in 1979. The Lomé Conventions are also worthy of mention as they gave preferential terms of entry to goods from 58 African, Caribbean and Pacific countries.

Some critics describe this period as one where the Community appeared to be out of control at times, characterised by excessive bureaucracy, by infighting and by interminable wrangling over spending on agriculture. It might even be said that the EC was losing sight of its goals. Moreover, the UK was showing distinct signs of under-enthusiasm. The lack of commitment from the UK was probably due in large measure to the revival during the Thatcher/Regan era of the "special relationship" with the United States. It should also be said, however, that a similar relationship exists between France and Germany. While both are fully committed to European integration, much more so than the UK for example, the very closeness of their relationship has given rise to the suggestion that these two countries are driving Europe forward in accordance with their own Franco-German agenda.

With the arrival of Jacques Delors as the new President of the European Commission in January 1985, the Community soon regained whatever momentum it had lost.

The impact of Jacques Delors

Delors made it clear that he was keen to make progress on issues which had been left in abeyance for some years. Above all he wanted to progress towards a more thorough-going union of member states. On taking up his post, Delors visited member countries to make himself known and to sound out opinion on a package of four proposals. He revived the idea of monetary union and of a defence union. Both of these had been considered previously but without any substantial progress being made. He also proposed a reform of institutional structures and the completion of the internal market through the removal of the non-tariff barriers to trade.

Of these, the last-mentioned offered the best prospect for success as there was general support for deregulation and free competition. However, Delors took the view that completing the internal market implied major amendments to the EEC Treaty and it was this issue which threatened to derail the entire process. While all members were happy to support the establishment of the Single Market in principle, Britain and Denmark were not prepared to go beyond the opening of internal borders. They saw no need for the proposed revision of the Treaty. A split thus emerged with the UK and Denmark supporting the internal market only and the majority accepting the Delors view.

The eventual outcome – The Single European Act – was agreed at the Luxembourg summit at the end of 1985. Inevitably, it was based on a compromise, which probably went further than sceptics would have wished. At the same time, it fell short of an unequivocal commitment to European union, an idea which Mrs Thatcher had contemptuously dismissed as "airy-fairy". The main points of the Act can be summarised briefly as follows.

- The measures necessary to complete the internal market with free movement of persons, goods, money and services were to be in place by 31 December 1992. These included the harmonisation of technical and safety standards on the basis that goods acceptable in one member state must be acceptable in all.
- Small and medium-sized enterprises were to be freed from legal and bureaucratic restrictions.
- Monetary union was to be "progressively realised", though this was not legally binding.

- Through more efficient use of Community funds, economic disparities between the regions were to be reduced.
- Through the introduction of the "co-operation procedure", Parliament was given the power to amend legislation on second reading, though in most cases the Council retained the right to overturn such amendments.
- Co-operation in technological research was to be encouraged.
- Action was to be taken to improve the environment and to have damage rectified at source by the polluter.
- The Act contained a somewhat vague commitment to co-operation and consultation on foreign policy matters in order to increase the influence of the Community.

Ratification of the Act was completed during 1987. Referenda were required in both Ireland and Denmark in order to achieve this. In the UK, the House of Lords eventually consented after looking likely to rebel on the issue. On 1 January 1993 the Single European Market came into operation.

Delors was less successful, however, in linking the Single Act to other aims of the Treaty. When his proposals for closer union were discussed at the Milan European Council in June 1985, both the UK and Denmark expressed serious reservations. As we have seen, the British Prime Minister, Margaret Thatcher, went so far as to describe the idea as "airy-fairy". Both the UK and Denmark felt that the Delors proposals went too far. The Danes threatened to walk out of the Luxembourg summit as a result. Italy too threatened to walk out, though for the opposite reason. Delors had not gone far enough for Italian taste! In the event, the Delors proposals were significantly weakened – largely at the UK's instigation – in order to secure agreement. (Delors somewhat ruefully referred to this as the "Texas chainsaw massacre"!) Even so, the Single Act permitted signatories to go beyond the internal market – to establish, in effect, full economic and monetary union.

The logic of the package proposed by Jacques Delors was that the single market required measures to harmonise conditions of employment if people were to circulate as freely as goods, money and services. Harmonising conditions of employment meant agreement on such issues as minimum wage levels, conditions for part-time or temporary workers and maternity rights. These ideas were resisted by the UK. A series of non-binding proposals, the Social Charter, was presented by the Commission in 1989. Even though this represented no more than a declaration of intent, the UK opposed the idea. Subsequently, Britain refused to support the Action Programme. Even though only some 50% of the proposals which it contained were legally binding, and even though existing British legislation is already adequate in many areas, Britain refused to agree. A modified version of the Action Programme was presented to the Strasbourg European Council at the end of 1989 but Britain alone of the 12 refused to sign. Similarly, at Maastricht in 1991, the UK chose to opt out of the Social

Chapter of the Treaty on European Union. The British government's position has been that these measures will increase business costs, destroying jobs and making goods produced in the EU less competitive.

Maastricht and the European Union

The Treaty on European Union agreed at Maastricht in December 1991 gave the European Community a new name, which has since been formally adopted following ratification of the Treaty. This was by no means the only change. A timetable for monetary union was agreed with the final phase due to begin in 1999 at the latest. The UK refused to commit itself to monetary union arguing instead that this would mean a loss of control over monetary policy. How many countries will be in a position to participate in a single currency remains unclear, though it appears probable that less than half of the present membership will be able to meet the "convergence criteria" by 1999. A "two-speed Europe" thus appears likely at least in this area.

While non-participation in monetary union will enable the UK to retain a degree of control over the domestic economy, this will not necessarily mean that the "opt-out" is beneficial. It is quite conceivable that the exchange rate for the Pound will be adversely affected by the power of the ECU and that the downward trend of recent years will continue. It also seems likely that once a single currency is introduced, the financial markets in the UK will become less attractive to investors and dealers; indeed it is quite possible that Frankfurt or Paris will eventually replace London as the major money market in Europe.

As well as "opting out" of the final phase of monetary union, the UK refused to sign the Social Chapter of the Treaty which formalised the ideas put forward in the Commission's Social Charter and Action Programme in 1989 and for much the same reasons. The other members are, however, agreed on this matter. The wisdom of this decision remains to be proven. It is unclear whether the UK will benefit by attracting extra investment – particularly from outside the European Union – or if jobs will ultimately be lost through lack of investment.

Denmark too was able to negotiate an "opt out" from monetary union. Despite this, voters rejected the Treaty in a referendum held in the spring of 1992. This decision was reversed in a second referendum held the following year. It appears that concerns regarding a possible loss of sovereignty – particularly in respect of security policy – were the major contributory factor in the electorate's initial rejection.

Referenda were also held in Ireland and in France to confirm ratification. While the outcome of the vote in the latter produced only a small majority in favour, the Irish electors voted strongly for the Treaty. In the UK, where a referendum is not a constitutional requirement, the parliamentary vote resulted in a small majority in favour. Were a referendum to be held (as over EC membership in 1975), the outcome would be difficult to predict.

The controversies over the Social Chapter, over sovereignty issues and over monetary union have tended to overshadow other, less contentious, aspects of the Treaty. All citizens of member states are automatically citizens of the European Union itself. As such they have the right to vote in local and European elections when living in another member state. They may also claim the diplomatic protection of any other EU state, should they require to do so, in a part of the world where their country of origin has no diplomatic representation.

The signatories also pledged themselves to close co-operation on matters of home affairs and justice. With the removal of most border controls, this is of particular importance for efforts to combat organised crime, drug trafficking, illegal immigration and money laundering.

Another key feature of the Maastricht Treaty is the provision for an ombudsman, with whom citizens of the Union can raise cases of alleged maladministration, who will investigate the complaint and publish findings in report form. There is, however, no obligation for any action to be taken on the basis of an ombudsman's report.

Developments since Maastricht

The most striking feature has undoubtedly been a further expansion in membership with the accession of Austria, Sweden and Finland on 1 January 1995. The EU thus has not only gained three new members but has expanded into Scandinavia in much the same way as it expanded into the Mediterranean during the 1980s. Accession was, however, rejected by the Norwegian electorate for the second time, following a referendum in which issues of sovereignty and independence played a prominent part.

A further expansion into Mediterranean Europe – with the accession of Cyprus and Malta – seems likely enough, though the timing is by no means certain. Turkey too has long expressed a wish to join, though political issues remain to be resolved before membership can become a realistic possibility.

Within the EU, a new team of commissioners took office in January 1995, though not without a degree of controversy over the choice of a successor to Jacques Delors. The Belgian Jean-Luc Dehaene, the preferred candidate of both France and Germany, proved unacceptable to the UK, who vetoed his appointment on the grounds that his views were too federalist for British taste. It remains to be seen whether the eventual choice, the Luxembourger Jacques Santer, will prove to be less federalist in outlook.

A further controversial issue concerns the implementation of monetary union, to which the UK is in any case not committed. The agreed timetable proposed 1 January 1997 as the earliest date for the beginning of the final phase, with 1 January 1999 as the latest. It would appear that the former date is now over-optimistic, while there are serious doubts about the feasibility of the latter. In simple language it seems likely that only a small number of EU members will be economically healthy enough to satisfy the criteria for a move to full monetary union and the eventual introduction of a single currency.

During 1996 the Maastricht Treaty is due to be reviewed. It seems likely that this will be an appropriate opportunity to reconsider plans for monetary union. At the same time, the UK may well come under pressure from its partners to soften its opposition to the Social Chapter of the Treaty.

Activity

□ Taking the country chosen in the Activity in Chapter 1, consider the economic position of that country after the Second World War. Issues that should be considered include:

- the level of damage suffered as a result of the War;
- the extent of external debt;
- the country's economic priorities;
- political changes resulting from the war.

□ On completing this task, examine the country's economy today, in order to establish current trends in:

- employment;
- growth;
- inflation;
- external trade.

How successful has the country been?

□ Explain what economic and political changes have taken place since the War and try to identify what outside assistance the country has received.

□ List the political and economic groupings which your chosen country has joined. These could include NATO, EFTA, OECD, etc.

Chapter Three

The New Europe –
The European Union

In addition, information is given on electoral arrangements in those twelve countries which were members of the Union before the accession of Austria, Finland and Sweden on 1 January 1995.

During the 1950s a number of different bodies were created. These included the European Coal and Steel Community (ECSC), the European Economic Community (EEC) and the European Atomic Energy Authority (EURATOM). To all intents and purposes, they led separate existences and were administered independently of each other until the 1967 reforms placed them under one roof, as it were. The six institutions through which control is now exercised are:

- The European Commission (based in Brussels)
- The Council of Ministers (based in Brussels and Luxembourg)
- The Committee of Permanent Representatives (based in Brussels)
- The European Parliament (based in Strasbourg, Brussels and Luxembourg) and its permanent committees
- The European Court of Justice (based in Luxembourg)
- The Court of Auditors (based in Luxembourg)

Each of these will be considered in turn. In addition, the role of the Economic and Social Committee and of the European Investment Bank will be described briefly.

The European Commission

The European Commission fulfils roles which are both administrative and political. It might be described as a hybrid organization. Confusion exists about the work which it performs and about the true extent of Commission power. To a Euro-sceptic, the Commission might appear to be a somewhat distant, almost dictatorial bureaucracy. A Euro-enthusiast, on the other hand, might argue that the Commission acts as the "conscience" of the Union and the guardian of the European ideal.

Though it has no responsibility for policy formulation (this being the role of the Council of Ministers), the Commission draws up legislative proposals, once agreement on policy has been reached. Moreover, it has a major role to play in the legislative process itself, as the latter part of the chapter shows. As a result, it is easy for ordinary citizens to associate the Commission directly with European legislative measures, especially if these prove to be controversial, unpopular or difficult to understand. The experience of the UK since the 1980s certainly suggests this to be the case.

Although many opponents of Europe may believe that the Commission is an enormous organization, this is hardly the case. In reality, it has a total staff of approximately 15,000 (at the time of writing). Although this is clearly a substantial figure, many government departments in the UK – and in other European countries – employ significantly more. Because these employees are drawn from all EU member states, the composition of the Commission can be said to be truly multinational.

The best known of these are the Commissioners themselves. Present arrangements are that each of the five largest states by population (Germany, France, the UK, Italy and Spain) provides two Commissioners and the smaller members one each. From January 1995, the UK has been represented by Sir Leon Brittan (Conservative) and Neil Kinnock (Labour). Although appointed by national governments, Commissioners are not supposed to promote the interests of their countries of origin; instead they should serve the European Union. These Commissioners are responsible for the work of 23 departments, often known as Directorates General. The

Directorates General resemble the different branches of the Civil Service in a country such as the UK.

Broadly speaking, the European Commission is responsible for the drafting of proposed legislation, the implementation of agreed policy and legislation and the administration of the European Union's finances. Because of its relatively small size, the Committee often delegates the actual implementation of European law to individual member governments, although it retains responsibility for ensuring that measures are carried out as intended and within the agreed time frame.

The need to delegate to national governments means that it is easy enough for opponents of Europe to portray the Commission as issuing orders from the safety of Brussels which override domestic institutions and established democratic practices. This impression may often be reinforced by the manner in which that is done. Delegation can take the form of a Directive, which specifies the result to be achieved (perhaps a safety standard for equipment or a qualitative requirement for food and drink), although member governments are allowed considerable scope in taking whatever measures they consider necessary to achieve the desired result within the time specified. Of the measures which the Commission is empowered to initiate, Directives are probably the best known – and almost certainly the least popular, probably because implementation is left to national governments. It can thus appear that Brussels has issued orders from afar. Moreover, non-compliance can lead to prosecution in the European Court of Justice.

A Regulation, on the other hand, is binding in its entirety and directly applicable in all member states. A Decision is usually addressed to one or more member states, upon whom it is directly binding. This approach is most likely to be used when some member states already have agreed measures which satisfy European standards, while others have not yet done so. Another possibility is that of a Recommendation or Opinion. As the terms suggest, these are merely the expression of a view or a suggested course of action. However, neither can be considered binding in a legal sense. In other words, the Commission is only empowered to legislate within an agreed framework and cannot impose legislation in a wilful or arbitrary fashion upon European Union members. Nevertheless, in the event of non-compliance, it is empowered to initiate legal proceedings.

The EEC Treaty committed signatories to the development of common European policies in a variety of areas. A major part of the Commission's work thus concerns monitoring progress where policy is already agreed, as well as ensuring that policies operate smoothly.

Finally, under Article 113 of the Treaty, the Commission has responsibility for the European Union's external trade relations. This may involve either participation in a formal negotiation process, as in the case of the 1993 GATT agreement, or less formal exchanges of views. In this respect it is worthy of note that while the Commission represented the interests of the

EU as a whole in the GATT negotiations mentioned above, individual members also participated in this process in their own right.

The Council of Ministers

If the Commission concerns itself with issues which can be broadly termed European, an important function of the Council of Ministers is to ensure that the governments of individual member states have ample opportunity to make their views and priorities known. Elected governments thus have a genuine say in the formulation of European Union policy.

Perhaps the term Council is not entirely appropriate in this case. What is known as the Council of Ministers is not one single body but a series of councils, the composition of which will vary according to the issue under consideration. If, for example, agricultural matters are being discussed, members will normally be represented by the minister responsible for agriculture. Similarly, if the foreign affairs are under consideration, foreign ministers will participate.

Although three meetings per year are held in Luxembourg, the bulk of Council business is conducted in Brussels. The frequency of such meetings depends naturally on the number and complexity of those matters requiring discussion or resolution. The number of meetings will inevitably vary from year to year. In 1984, for example, 80 Council meetings were held in all. Of these, 17 were devoted to foreign affairs, generally considered to be a high priority issue, while 14 concerned the vexed question of agriculture.

The Council might well be termed the powerhouse of the European Union. Policy decisions, without which there can be no legislation, are taken by the Council, which also has the final say in the legislative process. A law cannot be implemented, even if it has successfully completed all other stages in the legislative process, without the Council's final approval. Similarly, the Council is under no obligation to act upon amendments to draft legislation put forward by other institutions involved in the process, such as the European Parliament.

The Presidency of the Council is held by each member country in turn for a period of six months (1 January–30 June and 1 July–31 December) with at least one European Council taking place during each Presidency. Thus at least two European Councils will take place each year. During that period the minister from the country holding the Presidency will chair meetings of the Council. The tenure of the Presidency enables each country in turn to exert a degree of influence over the agenda. During the last British Presidency in the second half of 1992, for example, significant emphasis was placed on accelerating the pace of deregulation (a matter of particular importance to the British Government) in preparation for the Single European Market, which came into operation on 1 January 1993.

However, the Presidency also means that the incumbent country has responsibility for ensuring that unresolved issues are dealt with. One of the key issues which arose during the 1992 British Presidency involved the search for a solution to the difficulties raised by the rejection of the Maastricht Treaty by the Danish electorate earlier in the year.

During their country's tenure of the Presidency, ministers become spokespersons for the Union as well as for their country. This enables them to play an enhanced role in terms of influence and prestige. It seems likely that the smaller member states draw particular benefits from the office. The Government of the Republic of Ireland appears to have made effective use of the increased influence during its tenure of the Presidency (in 1990) to secure the release of an Irish citizen held hostage in Lebanon.

Heads of government from all EU member states meet less frequently than ministers in Council, though this in no way prevents bilateral contracts. While there was no provision in the Treaty of Rome for European summitry, heads of government did meet on a irregular basis during the 1960s. At the Paris summit in 1974, a decision was taken to formally institutionalise these gatherings, which are now known as the European Council. At that time, leading figures, such as President Valery Giscard d'Estaing of France and Chancellor Helmut Schmidt of West Germany saw a need for stronger leadership in the development of common policies and for a forum in which heads of government would meet on a regular basis to exchange ideas. The purpose of such meetings is usually to seek agreement on general principles rather than on the specific detail of individual policies. Since 1984, heads of government have held such summits at least twice yearly – sometimes more frequently. Heads of government meet at a suitable venue in the country holding the Presidency. During Britain's half year tenure of the Presidency in 1992, for example, two European Councils were held – the first in Birmingham and the second in Edinburgh.

The Committee of Permanent Representatives

This body – often known by its French acronym COREPER – consists of permanent officials drawn from each member state. Its perceived import-ance is indicated by the fact that its members have the rank of ambassador. In broad terms, COREPER has two functions. The first of these is to scrutinise legislative proposals emanating from the European Commission, in order to determine areas where there is already – or is likely to be – agreement and those which might prove divisive.

The Council of Ministers, which does not meet in permanent session, has only very limited opportunity for detailed discussion and scrutiny of proposed legislation. This function is fulfilled by COREPER which has a number of specialised committees for that purpose. With the detailed work completed elsewhere, the Council of Ministers can concentrate on more general issues, such as the definition of policy. COREPER thus serves both the Council of Ministers and the European Commission in a vital capacity by dealing with time-consuming matters of detail and identifying potential problem areas.

The European Parliament

Although the term "Assembly" was used in the original treaties, this was changed to "Parliament" in the early 1960s. While there was treaty provision for direct election of members, MEPs were actually appointed by national parliaments to serve in Strasbourg until 1979, when the first direct elections were held. Over the years the European Parliament has clearly gained in influence, yet today many commentators still see it as a somewhat toothless institution, a debating chamber rather than a dynamic centre where major decisions are made. As Figure 3.3 shows, Parliament's role was originally conceived as largely consultative and in many respects it remains so today. The opinion of Parliament was sought, though MEPs had little scope to exert real influence over policy. To some extent, with the passing of the Single European Act and the introduction of the Co-operation Procedure for certain legislation, this has been changed. (See Figure 3.4). Nevertheless, it can still be argued that the European Parliament remains isolated to a significant extent.

Although Parliament exercises a degree of democratic control and guarantees accountability, it has no power to initiate its own legislation other than on budgetary matters, nor does it take the final decision in actually passing European laws. In this sense, its powers are restricted when compared to, say, Westminster. Parliament may now have the right to amend legislative proposals, or to reject them, but even so the Council of Ministers has the power to overrule or disregard Parliamentary decisions.

In one area, however, the European Parliament is – at least in theory – able to exercise considerable power. This concerns the European Union's budget. In much the same way as the Chancellor in the UK requires Parliamentary approval before his budgetary proposals can be implemented, the budget of the European Union must be presented to the Strasbourg Parliament, which may reject it. Rejection of the budget could, naturally enough, have serious consequences for major areas of expenditure, such as the Common Agricultural Policy or the Regional Development Fund. However, this power (effectively a veto) has only been used once so far (in 1979), though during the 1980s MEPs delayed the issue of the budget on three occasions.

Commissioners are ultimately answerable to Parliament in the sense that they attend plenary sessions and committee meetings and answer oral questions. More importantly, Parliament has the power to dismiss Commissioners *en bloc* (though not individually!) – subject to a two-thirds majority. However, it has no say in the choice of replacements. Theoretically, therefore, national governments might choose to reinstate the self same body of Commissioners who had just been dismissed.

Plenary sessions (lasting for one week per month) take place in Strasbourg, the location most usually associated with parliamentary activity. However, for reasons of proximity to the European Commission, committee business (two weeks per month) is normally conducted in Brussels, while the administration is based in Luxembourg. MEPs and parliamentary staff thus spend considerable time travelling from one European location to another. In addition, MEPs are faced with travel to and from their constituencies.

In the Parliament, MEPs are seated not according to their country of origin but according to their political allegiance. The larger political groupings, such as the Socialists, thus may comprise MEPs from all member states. The present composition of the European Parliament is shown below in Figure 3.1.

Figure 3.1 Political Groups represented in the European Parliament after the 1994 elections include:

> EDA–European Democratic Alliance
> EPP–European People's Party
> ER–Technical Group of the European Right
> Ind–Not-aligned
> LDR–Liberal Democratic and Reformist Group
> LU–Left Unity
> RBW–Rainbow Group
> PES–Group of the Party of European Socialists.

Of the British political parties represented at Strasbourg, Labour MEPs are members of the Group of the Party of European Socialists (PES). The Conservatives participate in the European People's Party (EPP), while the Liberal Democrats are members of the Liberal Democratic and Reformist Group (LDR). The Scottish Nationalist MEPs belong to the Rainbow Group (RBW).

The MEPs from Northern Ireland are affiliated as follows:

OUP   –   European People's Party
DUP   –   Independent
SDLP   –   Group of the Party of European Socialists

The 16 MEPs from the Republic of Ireland belong to five different groupings in the Parliament. They are affiliated as follows:

Fianna Fail (7)   – European Democratic Alliance (EDA)
Fine Gael (4)   – European People's Party (EPP)
Labour (1)   – Group of the Party of European Socialists (PES)
Green Party (2)   – Greens
Independent (1)   – Rainbow Group (RBW)

Seats at Strasbourg are allocated to members states according to population. As the most populous state in the European Union, Germany has the largest number of seats and Luxembourg the smallest. The distribution of seats is shown below in Figure 3.2.

Figure 3.2 Seat distribution for the 1989 and 1994 European Elections:

	1989	1994
Germany	81	99
France	81	87
UK*	81	87
Italy	81	87
Spain	60	64
Netherlands	25	31
Portugal	24	25
Greece	24	25
Belgium	24	25
Denmark	16	16
Ireland	15	15
Luxembourg	6	6
Total	518	567

*For the elections in 1994, the UK's 87 seats were distributed as follows:
England   74
Scotland   8
Northern Ireland   3
Wales   5

With the accession of Austria, Sweden and Finland, the number of MEPs will increase to 626. Sweden will elect 22 MEPs, Austria 21 and Finland 16.

Electoral systems

The Treaty of Rome provided not only for the holding of direct elections but also for the use of a common electoral system in these elections, though without defining which electoral system was to be used. However, this has yet to be fully implemented. A proposal put forward by the European Parliament in 1982 was designed to introduce regionally based proportional representation (PR), in which seats would be allocated according to votes cast. Lack of agreement at governmental level has meant that, as yet, no unified electoral system operates.

Nevertheless, with the exception of Great Britain, all EU members have adopted Proportional Representation in one form or another for European elections. MEPs for constituencies in Northern Ireland are elected by proportional representation, using the Single Transferable Vote, while the remainder of the UK uses the same first-past-the-post system as for elections to Westminster, albeit with larger constituencies, covering in most cases seven or eight parliamentary seats.

Committees of the European Parliament

In all, 18 permanent committees exist. Their function is broadly similar to that of Parliamentary Committees in the UK. Like these, the Committees of the European Parliament conduct a significant amount of their business in public. Their purpose is to consider legislative proposals in detail and to prepare reports for presentation to Parliament. These can include recommendations for changes to the proposed legislation. The composition of each committee is designed to reflect the relative strengths of the different political groups. In other words, the membership should represent a rough cross section of European political opinion, as expressed at the last European election. Normally parliamentary committees meet in Brussels, although on occasion they have convened in other locations.

Existing committees cover such areas as: Budgetary Control; Environment, Regional Planning and Policy; Public Health and Consumer Protection; Women's Rights. Both the Council of Ministers and the European Commission are required to supply information requested by these committees and Commissioners (or their staff) frequently attend in person.

The European Court of Justice

The European Court of Justice (or ECJ), which is based in Luxembourg, should not be confused with other institutions not connected with the European Union but which have similar titles, such as the European Court of Human Rights (based in Strasbourg) or the International Court of Justice (which sits in The Hague).

The ECJ comprises 13 judges who serve a six year term of office. Each member state (12 before January 1995) puts forward one nomination, which is virtually guaranteed acceptance. The remaining judge is appointed on the basis of common consent. Appointees to the ECJ are exceptionally well-qualified legal experts whose expertise and independence are generally recognised.

The composition of the ECJ thus largely reflects the multinational make-up of the Union itself. Its function is to ensure that Treaties and laws are interpreted and implemented as intended and also to provide rulings where dispute has arisen. This is doubly important as European Law, where it exists, overrides or supersedes national legislation. Actions against members for non-compliance with European Directives are heard in the ECJ and it is difficult – though perhaps not entirely impossible – to imagine a scenario where any EU member government would deliberately defy an ECJ decision.

The Court of Auditors

Established under a 1975 Treaty (which came into force in 1977) and based in Luxembourg, the Court of Auditors is responsible for ensuring that the European Union's finances have been properly managed and adequate records (of revenue and expenditure, for example) maintained. As a result of this, the Court produces regular reports on routine financial matters for the Commission. As well as this, it reports on other issues concerning the administration of the Union's financial affairs. In November 1994, for example, the Court of Auditors investigated instances of alleged fraud involving an apparently widespread misuse of subsidies granted under the Common Agricultural Policy.

Currently, each member state appoints one official to serve on this Court. Appointees must have appropriate qualifications in auditing. As with judges sitting in the ECJ, appointments are made for a six year term. The 12 choose one of their number to serve a three year renewable term as President.

The Economic and Social Committee

The Economic and Social Committee (often shortened to ECOSOC or ESC) has no actual decision-making or legislative power; its function is purely consultative. Members are nominated by governments, subject to approval by the Council of Ministers. It owes its existence to a provision of the Treaty of Rome for a consultative forum, in which interest groups are able to articulate their views independently.

Membership comprises representatives of industry and commerce, the Labour movement and other groups, such as consumer organizations or environmentalists. They express their opinions and concerns, most notably to the European Commission, on a wide variety of issues, such as transport or social policy. Although in some cases consultation with ECOSOC is a statutory requirement, the influence which it is able to exert is extremely limited. For this reason, it is often viewed as little more than a talking shop.

The European Investment Bank

The European Investment Bank (or EIB) is acknowledged to be the largest single contributor of loan capital for development purposes within the European Union. In this process the EIB and the European Regional Development Fund (ERDF) can be seen as the key players and their functions as largely complementary. The bank is an important instrument of the EU's regional policy.

The EIB was established in 1958 in accordance with Articles 129–130 of the EEC Treaty and it has its headquarters in Luxembourg. All members of the European Union are *de facto* members of the EIB. The bank is financed in part by direct contributions made by its members and partly by borrowing activities on money on the markets of Europe and overseas.

Although funds are available for development projects elsewhere in the world, the vast bulk of EIB lending (an estimated 90%) is concentrated on the countries of the EU itself. Broadly speaking, projects must satisfy two sets of criteria in order to qualify for EIB support – and even then it is highly unlikely that the bank will agree to provide more than half of the estimated capital requirement. In this sense, the EIB can be seen to work in concert with other financial institutions, such as commercial banks. At the same time, this lessens the risk of vulnerability through over-exposure.

The first requirement is that the project must fall within the scope of Article 130 of the Treaty of Rome. This means that it must be seen to be of benefit to one or more of the less prosperous regions of the European Union – possibly by providing finance for infrastructure improvements or for the modernisation of industry (and thus improving competitiveness). Alternatively, there should be some tangible benefit to one or more members of the EU – or perhaps even to the Union as a whole – as, for example, in the case of expenditure on projects with environmental objectives.

Moreover, any loans made must be backed by adequate financial guarantees – not least because the EIB (unlike the IMF or the IBRD) raises the majority of its lending capital on the money markets rather than through the subscriptions of its members. For this reason, the European Investment Bank needs to ensure that not only is the project worthwhile in an objective sense but also that it represents a financially viable investment. There are obvious similarities between the lending policy of the EIB and those of more conventional financial institutions, such as commercial banks.

The distribution of power in the European Union

While Euro-sceptics tend to perceive the European Commission as an almost omnipotent organization, this view is seriously misplaced. It is, of course, true that the Commission has a major say over the content of

European law. Furthermore, it is the task of the Commission to actually draft legislation. The Commission is also the source of Directives, Decisions and Regulations, some of which have proved to be unpopular in the UK. However, in reality the Commission has little scope for independent initiative. The proposals which it is empowered to make depend on prior policy decisions made by the Council of Ministers, although it appears to enjoy a degree of licence as to how these may be interpreted. This is well illustrated by the experience of the late 1980s.

When Commission President Jacques Delors unveiled his plans for achieving Treaty goals which had been left largely in abeyance, they encountered determined opposition from the UK in the Council of Ministers. The net result of this was that, although Delors' plans derived directly from a commitment given by all signatories to the Treaty, British opposition in the Council meant that a large part of the Delors' plan had to be shelved for the time being. In other words, the scope for action which the European Commission undoubtedly has is dependent upon and is also clearly limited by the policies of the Council of Ministers. The decision-making cycle shows that no law can be made without Council agreement on policy initially, even if the drafting of legislative proposals is the responsibility of the Commission. Furthermore, it is the Council of Ministers which has the final and decisive say as to whether any proposal is enacted.

The influence of the European Parliament is by any objective standards severely restricted. Unlike national parliaments, it has only the most limited scope for law-making. While constraints on the activities of an unelected assembly are quite justifiable, it appears strange that they should remain after the introduction of direct elects to Strasbourg. As a result, the EP is still more of a consultative body than a powerhouse.

It is, of course, true that Parliament has the power to call Commissions to account and even to vote for their dismissal, though it would be powerless to prevent their immediate reinstatement. Similarly, while Parliament may amend legislative proposals, it has no means of ensuring that such amendments are accepted.

Real power in the European Union clearly resides in the Council of Ministers. It is the Council which begins the process of law-making by agreeing policy. It also has a significant input into the law-making process itself and, most importantly, it has the last word before proposals become law. The Council is under no obligation to accept amendments proposed by Parliament. If the Parliament may be said to "police" the European Commission, there is as yet no institution, or combination of institutions, which exercises a similar power over the Council of Ministers.

Britain's uneasy relationship with Europe, which is often blamed on excessive zeal on the part of an insensitive, unaccountable European Commission may, in fact, be no more than a reflection of its inability or unwillingness (or both!) to put its case adequately in the Council of Ministers. It is politicians, above all, who seek to apportion most blame to the Commission, just as it is politicians who apparently fail to make an impact at Council level.

How are decisions made?

The voting arrangements in the different institutions are described below.

European Commission: a simple majority is required.

Council of Ministers: the voting system used depends on the perceived importance of the issue under consideration. In many cases, a simple majority is sufficient. A growing number of issues are resolved by qualified majority whereby the votes of members are "weighted" roughly according to the size of the countries. Before the accession of Sweden, Austria and Finland, a qualified majority represented 54 weighted votes out of a possible 76. One important feature of this arrangement was that the five largest states were thus unable to out-vote the seven smaller members.

Qualified majority voting in the Council of Ministers, for all its merits, is often misunderstood in the UK. Euro-sceptics portray the increasing use of the qualified majority as a surrender of British sovereignty because it reduces the scope for the use of the veto. However, this applies in exactly the same measure to all other members. If British sovereignty has indeed been curtailed, so has that of France, of Germany or of Ireland in exactly the same way.

On a small and diminishing number of issues unanimity is required. In this case, abstentions are not counted so unanimity refers only to those actually casting their votes. It seems likely that the number of issues on which decisions are made in this way will continue to diminish as membership grows and unanimity becomes correspondingly more difficult to achieve.

European Parliament: on most issues, a simple majority of those voting is sufficient. However, if Parliament wishes to exercise its power to dismiss all 20 Commissioners, then a two-thirds majority is necessary. Since the first direct elections in 1979, Parliament has acquired a degree of legitimacy which had hitherto been lacking. MEPs can now be said to have a popular mandate for their parliamentary roles. The Co-operation procedure reflects this since measures passed by this method are presented twice to the Parliament, which has the power to either reject or amend on second reading. Following ratification of the Single European Act this more complex, though also more truly democratic, process is now increasingly used.

Legislative processes

Laws are generally made following one of two methods: the Consultation Procedure or the Co-operation Procedure. Of these, the former represents what might be called the traditional approach and has been used for most of the European legislation now in place. As Figure 3.3 shows, this method is relatively straightforward. The most significant feature is that while the other decision-making institutions are involved at least twice, Parliament has only one opportunity to make its position known. This reflects accurately the almost entirely consultative function of Parliament prior to the institution of direct elections in 1979. The Consultation Procedure has yet to be withdrawn; indeed a great deal of legislation still becomes law in this way.

How accessible is the decision-making process?

One of the commonest criticisms voiced in the UK is that the decision-making process appears somewhat remote and that individual citizens or even organised groups are largely unable to make their views known. However, this is an unduly pessimistic view.

Figure 3.3   The Consultation Procedure (simplified):

Council of Ministers agrees on policy

↓

Commission makes legislative proposals

↓

Parliament debates (may amend)

↓

Commission takes a view

↓

Council makes final decision

Figure 3.4 The Co-operation Procedure (simplified):

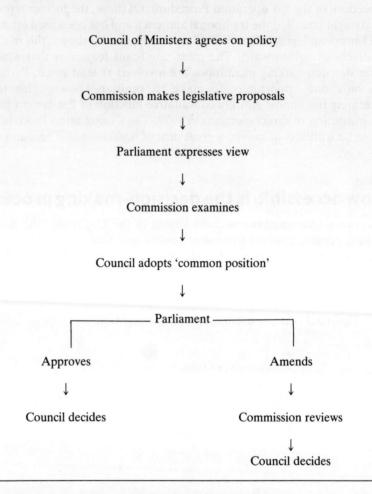

Council of Ministers agrees on policy

↓

Commission makes legislative proposals

↓

Parliament expresses view

↓

Commission examines

↓

Council adopts 'common position'

↓

─── Parliament ───

Approves   Amends

↓   ↓

Council decides   Commission reviews

                                  ↓

                             Council decides

Individuals in the UK know that their constituency MP can raise issues on their behalf with government departments and, if need be, with ministers themselves. The European decision-making process can be approached in much the same way. On behalf of their constituents, Westminster MPs are able to make their views known to members of the government, who, if they think appropriate, can bring the matter to the attention of the Council of Ministers. In certain cases, an approach can be made directly to the Cabinet Minister concerned. Alternatively, a lobby of Parliament could be organized either by individuals or interest groups. The Council of Ministers is the institution with the most influence, so an approach to the Council might seem the most appropriate. However, it should be borne in mind that

Council business is concerned mainly with the general principles of policy rather than the detailed discussion. Any attempt to influence Council thinking should, therefore, be couched in general terms.

A direct approach to an MEP might ensure that the issue is raised in the European Parliament – either in a plenary session or, more likely, in committee. While the influence of the EP – if clearly more extensive than in the past – is still limited, neither the Council of Ministers nor the Commission can, in reality, afford to disregard its views altogether.

While ordinary citizens can have little prospect of success if they approach the Commission as individuals, a unified approach by an organized group (preferably from more than one country), such as the members of trade associations, is more likely to secure a hearing in Brussels. The Commission is responsible, as we have seen, for preparing drafts of legislative measures, such as Directives. A well thought out approach at this stage of the process would at least ensure that the views of those directly concerned by the measure are taken into consideration.

For a significant number of measures, the views of ECOSOC, the Economic and Social Committee, must be sought. By virtue of the composition of this Committee, business people, union members and others have an opportunity to make their opinions known.

What the above shows is that individuals and organizations are not entirely without means of expressing their views, although for ideological reasons opponents of European integration often choose to suggest that this is not the case. The choice of the most appropriate institution to approach will depend obviously on the circumstances. While an approach to a combination of institutions may well increase the prospect of success, this would also prove more time-consuming and expensive.

Conclusion

The network of institutions may appear complex at first glance. This is perhaps why it is not well understood. The institutions which do most to shape the business environment in Europe are those involved directly in policy decisions or in law-making – the Council of Ministers, the European Commission and the European Parliament. The ECJ clearly also has a role to play in making judgements on points of law and in hearing cases where European law has been breached. Of these four, the Council of Ministers is by some way the most powerful, although its influence is often understated in the UK – not always by accident.

The decision-making process can be accessed by organizations or by individuals at various points in the cycle, although this is likely to be a time-consuming process and would require careful preparation. Nevertheless, despite the claims made by many Euro-sceptics, citizens of the European Union can make their views known. The major institutions involved in law-making are thus less remote than their critics would have us believe.

The other institutions discussed in this chapter, such as ECOSOC, the Parliamentary Committee and the Court of Auditors carry out most of their duties behind the scenes, though this does not necessarily mean that they are devoid of influence.

Electoral arrangements and voter participation

Belgium (Voting compulsory)

25 MEPs are elected (14 for Flanders, ten for Wallonia, one for the German speaking region). Belgium uses a PR system based on three regional lists presented by parties. Electors may vote for a list in its entirety or add or delete names of individual candidates.

Turnout in European Elections:

1979	–	91.4%
1984	–	92.2%
1989	–	90.7%
1994	–	90.7%

Denmark (Voting voluntary)

Denmark elects 16 MEPs using list-based PR. For this, the entire country is treated as one constituency. As in Belgium, votes can be cast for a complete party list. Voters may add or deselect individual candidates.

Turnout in European Elections:

1979	–	47.8%
1984	–	52.3%
1989	–	46.1%
1994	–	52.9%

France (Voting voluntary)

France's 87 MEPs are elected using list-based PR. For European elections, France is treated as one constituency (ie. lists are national). Seats are allocated in proportion to votes received subject to a 5% threshold.

Turnout in European Elections:
1979	–	60.7%
1984	–	56.7%
1989	–	48.7%
1994	–	52.7%

Germany (Voting voluntary)

99 MEPs are elected using list-based PR. The country is divided into 16 regional constituencies for which parties produce lists of candidates. Seats are allocated according to the share of the vote obtained but a 5% threshold applies.

Turnout in European Elections:
1979	–	65.7%
1984	–	56.8%
1989	–	62.4%
1994	–	60.0%

NB. The turnout figures for the electors in 1979, 1984 and 1989 refer to former West Germany only.

Great Britain (Voting voluntary)

The UK mainland elects 84 MEPs for single-member constituencies using a first-past-the-post system.

Turnout in European Elections:
1979	–	32.6%
1984	–	32.6%
1989	–	36.2%
1994	–	36.4%

Greece (Voting compulsory)

Greece elects 25 MEPs using a list-based system of PR. For this purpose the entire country is treated as a single constituency.

Turnout in European Elections:		
1984	–	77.2%
1989	–	79.9%
1994	–	71.2%

Ireland (Voting voluntary)

15 MEPs are elected using PR based on the Single Transferable Vote. The country is divided into four constituencies.

Turnout in European Elections:		
1979	–	63.6%
1984	–	47.6%
1989	–	68.3%
1994	–	44.0%

Italy (Voting voluntary)

87 MEPs are elected using PR with party lists. The country is divided into five regional constituencies and seats are allocated according to the share of the vote in each region. Voters may choose individual candidates as well as parties.

Turnout in European Elections:		
1979	–	85.5%
1984	–	83.9%
1989	–	81.5%
1994	–	74.8%

Luxembourg (Voting compulsory)

Luxembourg elects six MEPs using list-based PR with the whole country considered to be one constituency.

Turnout in European Elections:		
1979	–	88.9%
1984	–	88.8%
1989	–	87.4%
1994	–	86.6%

Netherlands (Voting voluntary)

31 MEPs are elected using a list-based system of PR. The country is treated as a single constituency. Therefore seats are allocated according to the share of the national vote obtained.

Turnout in European Elections:		
1979	–	57.8%
1984	–	50.6%
1989	–	47.2%
1994	–	35.6%

Northern Ireland (Voting voluntary)

Unlike the rest of the UK, Northern Ireland elects its three MEPs for one single constituency using PR based on the Single Transferable Vote.

Turnout in European Elections:		
1979	–	not known
1984	–	47.6%
1989	–	47.7%
1994	–	48.7%

Portugal (Voting voluntary)

25 MEPs are elected using the list-based system of PR, in which the whole country is treated as one constituency.

Turnout in European Elections:

1987	–	68.9%
	(first elections following accession)	
1989	–	51.2%
1994	–	35.5%

Spain (Voting voluntary)

Spain elects 64 MEPs using list-based PR. For this, the country is treated as one constituency. Seats are therefore allocated according to the share of the national vote obtained.

Turnout in European Elections:

1987	–	68.9%
	(first elections following accession)	
1989	–	54.6%
1994	–	59.1%

Activity

☐ Your chosen country has decided to become a member of the European Union. How would it set about this task? Are there any alternatives to full membership?

☐ An application to join the EU will need the support of existing members. Which members appears most likely to support your country's application?

☐ Which individuals or groups will it need to convince within each country in order to gather the necessary level of support?

☐ Is membership of the EU likely to conflict with membership of other organizations which your country has already joined?

☐ How would it go about making an application?

☐ What information will the country need to supply in support of its application?

☐ How do you think the EU members will react to the application?

☐ In particular, which issues could prove difficult to resolve?

Chapter Four

Non-Eu Institutions

Aim of this chapter

□ To outline the purpose of institutions (such as the European Court of Human Rights and the International Court of Justice), which have similar sounding titles to EU institutions

□ To identify non-EU institutions located in Europe, of which many (though not necessarily all) EU countries are members

□ To enable the reader to differentiate between those institutions which are part of the European Union and those which are not

Chapter Three is devoted to the major institutions of the European Union, their roles and responsibilities. There are, however, other organizations which in various ways can influence the business environment in the EU – even if these are not actually part of the Union itself. A degree of confusion does exist as to the purpose and function of many of these and this is compounded to some extent by their titles and by their locations. Some of these may have a close relationship with the EU and it is, therefore, all too easy for the non-expert to assume that they too are part of the European Union's institutional structure. This chapter is devoted to seven institutions, which could come into the above category.

● The European Free Trade Association (EFTA)
● The European Economic Area (EEA)
● The Council of Europe

- The European Trade Union Confederation (ETUC)
- The Organization for Economic Co-operation and Development (OECD)
- The European Court of Human Rights (ECHR)
- The International Court of Justice (ICJ)

One section is devoted to each of the above in turn. For historical reasons, it might be argued that EFTA should be considered alongside the EU. However, because it is – and always has been – a separate organization, it seems more appropriate to include it in this chapter. While all EU members participate in the EEA, it also has members from outside. It therefore seems wiser to include the EEA in this chapter rather than in the previous one. Two of the organizations listed above (the ICJ and the OECD) are not exclusively European in character. Nevertheless, they are included here because they are both based in Europe and because the latter in particular does have substantial prestige and influence.

The European Free Trade Association (EFTA)

As the previous chapter showed, EFTA was created largely at the instigation of the UK. It was intended to rival, perhaps even upstage, the emergent EEC. The idea stems from the original British proposal for a free trade area covering much of Western Europe. Britain, unwilling to countenance many of the features of the EEC, preferred a much looser structure. Members would trade freely with each other but without any commitment to "ever closer union", or to common policies as embodied in the Treaty of Rome.

Though the original British idea of a large free trade area did indeed generate a degree of interest among potential members, it encountered stiff opposition from France in particular. EFTA had no need for the complex institutional structure which has arguably weakened its rival quite seriously. The absence of a common external tariff and a unified agricultural policy explain at least in part why administrative arrangements were not felt necessary. Moreover, EFTA, unlike the EEC, lacked any semblance of a political dimension. The EFTA Treaty contains no commitment to the development of common policies or to the joint administration of key industries (as in the case of the ECSC). In other words, there was very little which required administration.

The idea, which might be described as free trade without encumbering political strings accords well with the traditional British adherence to free trade *per se*, as well as its *laisser-faire* notion that the market should be left to regulate itself, or that too much government is bad government. It should also be said that these two had served Britain well in the past. Clearly any British-inspired organization (especially one which might conceivably have put the upstart EEC in its place) would draw heavily on British beliefs and traditions. However, the lack of a political dimension and of administrative structures reflect not only long-held British beliefs but also EFTA's original composition, which is of considerable significance.

Among the founder members, there was a strong tradition of neutrality (typified by Switzerland, Sweden and Austria). Although neutrality can, of course, be interpreted in a variety of ways, it does restrict participation in many international organizations – especially when these organizations are perceived as constituting a political alliance or as having a clear political dimension. EFTA thus was able to meet British objections to the EEC, while at the same time accommodating neutral states with their self-imposed lack of room for manoeuvre. The founder members of EFTA thus represent an interesting, if ill-balanced, collection of states. Apart from the UK, there was a strong Scandinavian presence (Sweden, Denmark and Norway) with two small neutral states from Central Europe (Austria and Switzerland) together with Portugal, a virtual political leper at that time, despite its long-standing friendship with the UK. Clearly, only a truly non-political organization would have been appropriate in the circumstances.

Given its origins, it was clear from the outset that EFTA depended heavily on the UK for prestige and influence. Therein lay a major problem: it is difficult to escape the impression that EFTA was created along essentially negative lines. Its lack of a common policy on external tariffs and on agriculture, the absence of political commitments and of administrative arrangements all correspond to British objections to the EEC. EFTA, in other words, was not intended as a constructive alternative; indeed it was the very opposite.

Whether EFTA could seriously have rivalled the EEC in economic terms seems highly debatable. For one thing, the disparity in population should be considered. With a population of rather less than 100 million, EFTA was roughly half the size of the EEC as then constituted. The UK alone accounted for roughly two-thirds of EFTA's total output (arguably for even more of its prestige in international terms) and EEC economies were growing much faster than that of the UK.

If EFTA was dependent on the UK for prestige, it might be argued that Britain did its partners a notable disservice. By applying for EEC membership so soon after establishing a rival organization, Britain, whether intentionally or not, had begun to undermine EFTA. The process of application, rejection and re-application in the early and mid-1960s can have done little to inspire confidence, particularly given the length of time involved. Above all, it raised questions about the firmness of the UK's commitment to EFTA.

Having been rejected once by the EEC (in the person of Charles de Gaulle), Britain still found it impossible to settle to life within the very organization which it had founded as an alternative. Other EFTA members, Norway and Denmark, chose to apply to the EEC at the same time as Britain. Within a matter of months since its creation, therefore, EFTA stood to lose almost half its membership. One of the problems facing EFTA has been the changes in membership since its establishment. Of the seven founder members:

- Denmark is now a member of the European Union
- the UK is now a member of the European Union
- Austria voted in 1994 to join the European Union
- Sweden voted in 1994 to join the European Union
- Norway (following rejection in 1972) voted in November 1994 to remain outside the European Union

---

Figure 4.1   EFTA Membership 1960–1994

EFTA founder members:	UK
	Austria
	Switzerland
	Portugal
	Sweden
	Norway
	Denmark
New members:	Finland (formerly associate member)
	Iceland
	Liechtenstein
Departures:	UK (1973)
	Denmark (1973)
	Portugal (1986)
	Sweden (1995)
	Finland (1995)
	Austria (1995)

Thus, of the original members, only Switzerland and Norway have remained within EFTA. Of those states which joined EFTA after 1960, Finland also voted in 1994 to join the EU. EFTA has experienced a high turnover in its membership though clearly the most serious damage which it has suffered was the departure of the UK. Without Britain, EFTA has appeared to lack both direction and influence. It might, therefore, be said that almost from the outset, the future of EFTA was in doubt. Membership has changed quite considerably during its lifetime, as EFTA countries have opted for membership of the European Union while others, such as Finland, Iceland and Liechtenstein have become full members of EFTA.

EFTA and the EEC/EC/EU have been able to co-exist in a relatively harmonious way. This may be because, after the departure of the UK, EFTA lost what economic capacity it had to be a serious rival to the EC. In any event, EFTA should be seen as a purely *commercial* organization, which was never intended to be anything else. EFTA's major aim has always been the liberation of trade.

The European Economic Area

Although EFTA has been weakened at different times by the departure of members, it has been strengthened in other respects by co-operating closely with the EU in order to liberalise trade between the two organizations. However, this might have been threatened by the Single European Market, to which EFTA states had no automatic right of access. Discussions between the two organizations were begun in 1984 and eventually led to agreement to create the European Economic Area (EEA). The EEA extended the Single European Market to include the seven EFTA states, thus establishing a trading area comprising 19 states with a total population approaching 400 million.

The EEA, as proposed, thus accounted for some 46% of world trade. It became operational on 1 January 1994. Of the 19 potential members, only 18 actually participated, however. In a referendum held in December 1992, Switzerland voted not to join. It would appear that nationalistic arguments and concerns about neutrality carried more weight with the electorate than the economic case for membership.

In many respects, the creation of the EEA can be considered a wise step for EFTA members. It secured access to the Single Market for countries in close geographical proximity. In any event, many of these, such as Austria, already had close trading relations with EU members, most notably with Germany.

It could also be argued, however, that in some respects, the EEA agreement worked against EFTA. EFTA members would become part of the Single Market with its integrated system of rules. Whatever the economic benefits which might accrue, there are also potential drawbacks. EFTA states would have to accept the Single Market rules as already established and could expect to exercise only limited influence over future developments. It seems likely that this may have helped to persuade some EFTA members that their best course was to pursue full membership of the European Union. Furthermore, EFTA members had no say over European Union policy and were isolated from the decision-making process. Participation in the EEA would thus leave EFTA states to some extent exposed to the vagaries of EU decision-making and with little input into the process.

The Council of Europe

Article 1 of the Statute of the Council of Europe states that its aim is to ". . . achieve a greater unity between its Members for the purpose of safeguarding and realising the ideals and principles which are their common heritage and facilitating their economic and social progress . . .". The sentiments expressed in the Council statute may appear to echo the Treaty of Rome which the statute predates in fact by some eight years. If there is still a degree of confusion as to the purpose of the Council of Europe, this may be due in part to its title and to the fact that its headquarters are in Strasbourg. However, the Council of Europe is concerned primarily – though by no means exclusively – with matters of human rights.

Figure 4.2 Membership of the Council of Europe with years of accession

Austria	1956	Liechtenstein	1978
Belgium	1949	Luxembourg	1949
Cyprus	1961	Malta	1965
Czechoslovakia	1991	Netherlands	1949
Denmark	1949	Norway	1949
Finland	1989	Portugal	1949
France	1949	San Marino	1988
Germany	1951*	Spain	1977
Greece	1949	Sweden	1949
Hungary	1990	Switzerland	1962
Iceland	1950	Turkey	1949
Ireland	1949	United Kingdom	1949
Italy	1949		

* 1951 is the year in which West Germany acceded to the Council of Europe

---

The Council of Europe consists of three institutions. These are the Committee of Ministers, the Consultative Assembly and the European Court of Human Rights (ECHR). Although it was responsible for the European Convention on Human Rights, the Council's powers are extremely limited; it acts more as a consultative forum where members discuss shared concerns and interests on human rights matters. The lack of legislative powers stemmed at least in part from British opposition, though governments of other member countries were also keen to restrict the Council's remit.

The European Trade Union Confederation

The ETUC acts as an umbrella organization for approximately 40 million trade union members from some 20 different countries, not all of whom are members of the European Union or of EFTA. The purpose of the ETUC might be seen as exerting what influence it can over European policy in order to safeguard the interests of its members. In this respect, it is somewhat handicapped in two important ways. Firstly to succeed in its purpose, the ETUC would need to engage in negotiation (or at least consultation) with European employers. However, there is no single body to which all European employers' organizations belong. Secondly, the European labour movement itself can hardly be described as unified. While confederations with differing values affiliate to the ETUC, ideological and other differences remain largely unresolved.

The spectrum of political opinion represented in the ETUC ranges from Christian Democracy to Communism. Similarly, the strength of the movement is uneven; indeed its numerical strength would appear to be in inverse proportion to the degree of ideological commitment displayed by confederations in different parts of the continent. In Scandinavia, relatively moderate confederations recruit strongly. In France, on the other hand, where the movement is more obviously ideologised, recruitment, while difficult to estimate accurately, is likely to be less than 20 per cent of the labour force. A North-South divide may thus be said to exist in terms of both recruitment and political stance.

As the previous chapter shows, the views of ECOSOC (the Economic and Social Committee) are sought on a variety of legislative matters. Within ECOSOC, the ETUC has the task of articulating the standpoint of the labour movement. However, because ECOSOC's role is consultative, the ETUC can do no more than express an opinion without any guarantee that this will influence the content or spirit of legislation. The ETUC thus acts largely as a co-ordinating body for the labour movement in Europe and as a forum where ideas can be exchanged. Although nominally it represents a significant proportion of the European labour force, the ETUC finds it difficult to exert meaningful influence over decision-making. To its critics (and these include many of its members), it is sometimes seen as no more than a European talking shop with little, if any, real power.

The Organization for Economical Co-operation and Development (OECD)

Although founded in 1961, the origins of the OECD can be traced back to the early post-war era. The Organization for European Economic Co-operation (OEEC) with 16 members was created in 1948 to assist with economic recovery. Perhaps most importantly, the OEEC played an important role in co-ordinating the European response to the Marshall Aid Programme by assessing needs for both goods and capital. In this regard it is worth remembering that the OEEC was an inter-governmental, as opposed to supranational, body and this may well help to explain why the United Kingdom played a key part, while refusing to become involved with organizations such as the ECSC.

By the end of the 1950s, with European recovery well under way, the objectives of the OEEC had largely been met. In response to this, and also to the establishment of the EEC, the Treaty of Paris in 1960 established the OECD with a significantly different focus of activity. In broad terms, the OECD concentrates on the achievement of three aims: the maximisation of sustainable economic growth; the economic expansion of members and non-members; the expansion of world trade on a non-discriminatory basis.

It is perhaps best known as a forum for the discussion of matters of economic policy among its members as well as for the regular publication of reports, economic statistics and forecasts. In recent years, the OECD has also turned its attention to environmental matters with studies on pollution and traffic congestion. It has also proved responsive to political change in the former Warsaw Treaty Organization countries and in 1990 it published a report highly critical of Western investment policy towards the new democracies of Eastern and Central Europe.

Although not strictly speaking a European organization in the same way as most of the others under consideration in Chapters Three and Four, the OECD clearly does have significant influence in Europe – not least because the majority of its members are European Countries.

Figure 4.3 Membership of the OECD

European Members (19):

Austria	Belgium
Denmark	Finland
France	Germany
Greece	Iceland
Ireland	Italy
Luxembourg	Netherlands
Norway	Portugal
Spain	Sweden
Switzerland	Turkey
United Kingdom	

Non-European Members (5):

Australia	Canada
Japan	New Zealand
United States	

Total membership 24

The European Court of Human Rights (ECHR)

This institution, which is based in Strasbourg, is often confused with the European Court of Justice. While the latter deals with the interpretation and implementation of European Union law, the ECHR decides on matters of human rights not merely in the European Union but in all those countries which have ratified the European Convention on Human Rights. The ECHR thus performs a similar function for the Council of Europe to that of the ECJ for the European Union.

Persons convicted of criminal or civil offences where human rights issues (such as the right to a fair trial) are at stake may appeal to the ECHR, once the domestic appeals procedure has been exhausted. Usually, such cases are heard first by the European Commission on Human Rights (not to be confused with the European Commission within the EU) who will reach a decision on the point at issue before the matter is referred to the Court itself. Normally, the ECHR will follow the decision of the Commission, though this should not necessarily be considered a foregone conclusion.

Judgments of the European Court of Human Rights can have the same implications for domestic legislation as those of the European Court of Justice. If the ECHR were to rule that, say, British law had not allowed a defendant a fair opportunity to present his or her case adequately, then Britain, having ratified the European Convention on Human Rights, would be under an obligation to change – or at least reinterpret the application of – the legislation in question.

The International Court of Justice (ICJ)

This institution sits in permanent session in The Hague. Its purpose is to settle legal disputes brought before it by countries (not by individual citizens) who have previously agreed to put their case to the Court and to abide by its decision. In so doing, the ICJ acts as the principal judicial body of the United Nations Organization. The Court comprises 15 judges who serve a nine year term of office. The judges themselves are chosen by the UN's Security Council and its General Assembly.

The ICJ might conceivably be asked to rule on such matters as fishing rights outside territorial waters or on a disputed border. While the European Court of Justice rules on matters involving European Union Law and the ECHR decides on human rights issues, the International Court can only arbitrate where points of international law are contested by two or more countries.

Conclusion

Most of the organizations discussed in this chapter are not connected directly to the European Union, although they all can have some influence on the European business environment. In some cases, however, this influence may be indirect.

The evolution of EFTA is closely linked to that of the EU – not least because so many of its members have joined the larger institution. EFTA remains a loosely structured organization which lacks the economic, political and social dimensions of the EU. It is a free trade area; it was never intended to be anything else. Nevertheless, whatever their differences in outlook, EFTA and the EU have established a *modus vivendi* through the establishment of the European Economic Area, which allowed those EFTA members who had not joined the EU to enjoy the economic benefits of the Single Market. Whether this means that the remaining EFTA members will themselves eventually accede to the EU appears doubtful at present – not least after the Norwegian referendum in late 1994 and also in view of Switzerland's rejection of the EEA. However, if the EU continues to expand, the consequences of remaining outside may well have to be re-assessed.

The influence of the ECHR and the ICJ is limited to legal matters in the sense that the decisions of either are binding. In the case of the Court of Human Rights this means that domestic legislation may have to be amended, if the human rights of individuals are found to have been curtailed.

Both the Council of Europe and the European Trade Union Confedera-tion can exercise little direct influence on the business environment as their role is largely consultative. Nevertheless, views expressed in or by either organization do carry some weight.

While the OECD does not make policy decisions as such or pass laws, its reports, forecasts and analysis are highly respected. It also plays an important role in the discussion of broad economic issues such as growth and the promotion of trade on a non-discriminatory basis. It seems likely that the OECD can thus influence economic policy in the EU – not least because all 15 EU members are also members of the OECD in their own right. This influence is also likely to be felt further afield.

Activity

□ Compile charts or tables showing those international institutions your chosen country has joined (with dates if possible) and those it has not.

□ Assess the reasons why the country has joined some and not others. These could be historical, political or economic, or a combination of these. Indeed, there could be other factors.

□ Has your country ratified the European Convention on Human Rights? If so, when? If not, why?

□ Has the OECD written reports or forecasts on your chosen country's economic performance? What conclusions were drawn?

□ Overall, assess the international awareness of the country and identify the areas in which it is willing to co-operate with other countries.

Chapter Five

The Economic and Commercial Environment

Aims of this chapter

- □ To explain how the various economies of Europe have developed and outline briefly how each individual economy is performing at the moment
- □ To consider the problems that have been uncovered and speculate on the likely future of the countries
- □ To identify the types of business unit in each country
- □ To consider the role of the central bank and name the main banks and recognise their roles
- □ To examine the importance of the stock exchange and investigate any other financial institutions
- □ To assess the place of the state in the commercial activities

Austria

There is public ownership of many basic industries, and state involvement in the engineering, vehicle, electrical and chemical sectors. The state has a majority shareholding in the two largest banks. About one-third of Austrian industry consists of subsidiary companies with overseas owners, including BMW, General Motors, Phillips and Sony.

Since about 1955, Austria enjoyed steady growth together with fairly low inflation and unemployment, making the country one of the most prosperous in the world. There was a slowing in the rate of growth in the early 1980s, but it picked up in 1987. The recession of the early 1990s had some effect on Austria, but rather less than many other countries, and inflation and unemployment have remained relatively insignificant. The country has gained from the collapse of Communism in Eastern Europe, as its position has allowed it to become a base for companies wishing to diversify into the East.

Types of company

- Gesellschaft mit beschränkter Haftung (GmbH) – a limited liability company.
- Aktiengesellschaft (AG) – a stock corporation.
- Genossenschaft – a co-operative.
- Offene Handelsgesellschaft (OHG) – a general partnership.
- Kommanditgesellschaft (KG) – a limited partnership.
- Gesellschaft mit beschränkter Haftung Kommanditgesellschaft (GmbH und Co. KG) – a limited partnership with a limited liability company as a partner. This is not commonly found in Austria.

Banks

The central bank is the Austrian National Bank, which controls the money supply, deals with international payments, outlines monetary policy and maintains the strength of the currency. The government has a majority holding in the two largest banks, Creditanstalt-Bankverein and Österreichische Länderbank. The other major banks are the Girozentrale and the Bank der Österreichischen Sparkassen AG, the Österreichische Kontrollbank and the Zentralsparkasse und Kommerzialbank. There are a large number of foreign banks in Austria, using Vienna as a base because of its proximity to eastern Europe. There are about 6,000 customers per bank, compared with 84,000 in the UK. This suggests that there are too many banks in the system.

The Stock Exchange

The Vienna Stock Exchange deals mainly in securities. Turnover is modest by western European standards. Share ownership is not widespread in Austria.

Belgium

There is a public ownership of some industries and, as the economy relies upon its export earnings, there is strong state support for industry. The main Belgian industries are steel, motor vehicles and textiles, but the country possesses few mineral resources, and has to import large quantities of fuel and raw materials. This means that exports are essential to pay for the imports, and in fact, 70% of Belgium's GDP is exported, leaving the country vulnerable to fluctuations in world trade. The oil crisis of the 1970s reduced profitability, and increased raw material and wage costs. Unemployment and inflation rose and the Government's economic policy attempted to maintain the purchasing policy of households, so public spending grew. However, in 1982, the Belgian franc was devalued, and an incomes policy introduced. Fiscal incentives were offered to assist business investment. This helped to improve competitiveness and curb inflation, but unemployment and public spending remained high.

From 1985, modernisation of monetary policy took place and as a result GDP improved, with major improvements in manufacturing investment. As with most European countries, the economy slowed down in the early 1990s and at the moment Belgium has relatively high unemployment, especially among unskilled workers. Productivity in Belgium has increased so that there is little demand for the unskilled. The social welfare system is well-developed and accounts for 40% of total central government expenditure. The high unemployment means increased social security benefits, and this problem will not readily disappear, but will continue to keep public spending high. Belgium contains the Headquarters of NATO and the EU which greatly assist the economy.

Types of company

- Société Anonyme/Naamloze Vennootschap – must have at least two founders, managed by a board of at least three directors, and usually the signature of two directors is needed for all company matters. It enjoys limited liability.
- Société Privée à Responsabilité Limitée/Besloten Vennootschap met Beperkte Aansparkelijkheis – is similar to a private company in the UK, and so cannot have a stock exchange listing.
- Société Co-opérative/Co-operative Vennootschap – a co-operative with limited liability (although Belgian law allows co-operatives to have unlimited liability).
- Sole traders – have no incorporation or public formalities but must be recorded on the Commercial Register.

Banks

The state bank is the National Bank of Belgium, which issues coins and notes, clears cheques for the commercial banks, and ensures the financial soundness of the country. There are over 80 commercial banks and many foreign banks trade in Belgium. The Générale Banque, the Banque Bruxelles Lambert and the Kredietbank have branches throughout the country. The state-owned ASLL-Bank, Gemeentekrediet/Crédit

Communal and NMKN/SNCI are financial institutions, but act as banks and have offices nationwide.

The Stock Exchange

The Brussels Stock Exchange is active, particularly at the moment, in short and medium term securities, and has a growing futures market.

Denmark

Until the Second World War, Denmark was neutral, but the German occupation ended this and Denmark was the first Scandinavian country to join the European Community, on 1 January 1973, along with the UK. There has been considerable state involvement in industry, but in recent years this has reduced as the government has engaged in a policy of privatisation.

The size of Denmark has forced firms to export but high labour costs means that Denmark has concentrated on quality products, where price is less important, eg. Danfoss thermostats, Grundfuss pumps, radiometer blood analysis apparatus dominates the world market. This has helped to create a prosperous country with a high standard of living.

The recession of the early 1990s had an impact on Denmark, bringing about rising unemployment and inflation and the position was not helped by the country's wide-ranging social welfare system which was particularly expensive at this time. In order to support this system, taxation is high and this reduces the ability to spend, but there have been reductions in the higher rates recently. To tackle the problems of the economy, in 1993 the centre-left coalition that was in power introduced a programme for reforms of economic and taxation policy, labour and education.

Types of company

- Public Limited Company.
- Private Limited Company.
- General Partnership.
- Limited Partnership.
- Sole trader.

Banks

The central bank is the Danish National Bank, which is responsible for a sound monetary system, though matters of principle are decided in conjunction with the government. The two major Danish commercial banks are Den Danske and Unibank with various smaller national and regional banks. The large number of commercial banks and savings banks has been much reduced by mergers. In 1991, Postal Giro was authorised to conduct banking activities, and was renamed Girobank.

As a result of the Commercial Banks and Savings Banks Act of 1974, the differences between the commercial and savings banks has narrowed greatly. Now, the commercial banks attract deposits from the public, as the savings banks had always done, and also offer their services to the public at large, rather than just trade and industry, while the savings banks are beginning to lend to firms more readily.

The Stock Exchange

Denmark has many small and medium sized firms which are normally financed by the banks. Nevertheless there are about 300 companies listed on the Copenhagen Stock Exchange. International issuers list bonds on the Copenhagen Stock Exchange, so securities constitute a vital element to the trade.

Finland

Free enterprise is the keystone of the Finnish economy. However, there is some state control – a monopoly on the manufacture, import and distribution of alcohol, and control of the railways, broadcasting and television (except commercial) and some companies in which it has a majority holding. Finland is a highly industrialised country, producing a wide range of industrial and consumer goods. Timber and associated products represent around 40% of the value of Finnish exports, and so the country is vulnerable to world fluctuations in demand for such products. The largest industrial sector is engineering, and although this is very efficient, it declined in the early 1990s and helped cause a serious recession. Another factor was the decline in the construction boom of the late 1980s. As the prices of Finnish-made materials were high, many were imported more cheaply, which compounded the decline in industry. The general recession of the early 1990s worsened the problems of the economy. The Finns have enjoyed an affluent lifestyle, with an elaborate social welfare system which accounted for almost a third of total general expenditure. The recession of the 1990s and the consequent increase in public spending on welfare brought about a budget deficit. Recovery is likely to be slow.

Finland, situated next to the Soviet Union, has always been in a vital strategic position, and so has always adopted a cautious foreign policy, so as not to offend its powerful neighbour. The changes in east-west relations may also affect Finland.

Types of company

- Limited liability companies (OY) are the most common form of company in Finland.
- Unlimited partnerships.
- Limited partnerships.
- Sole traders.

Banks

The central bank is the Bank of Finland, which is responsible for maintaining a stable monetary system and facilitating the circulation of money, and in consultation with the government exercises economic policy by its monetary and foreign exchange activities. There are three types of banks:

- Commercial Banks, which hold 46% of all banking deposits in Finland. The largest are Kansallis-Osake-Pankki and the Union Bank of Finland.
- Co-operative Banks with 28% of deposits. They are owned by their members, and largely serve wage and salary earners, but other customers include small business, especially agricultural and forestry.
- Savings Banks with 26% of deposits, which are deposit-taking institutions which operate as banks, but do not distribute profits. Customers tend to be households, professionals and smallish companies. The deposits of the largest, the Savings Bank of Finland, makes it the country's fourth largest bank.

The differences between the banks have almost disappeared as restructuring is taking place with mergers, branch closures and savings banks becoming limited companies.

The Stock Exchange

Foreign investors are becoming interested in the listed companies on the Helsinki Stock Exchange, probably because of the political stability of the country.

France

Central government has always played a crucial part in business activity. The post war years saw a series of Five Year Plans designed to assist economic growth. State ownership is considerable, and by 1984 the public sector represented over a third of investment and nearly a quarter of exports. The private sector is dominated by a handful of well-known industrialists and major firms, with a large number of small producers, as is demonstrated by the national average of 7.6 employees per firm. Labour, law and social security legislation is extensive and detailed and there are regulations concerning the organization of business in France, but business people are adept at seeking loopholes.

From 1958 to 1981, there was virtually uninterrupted one party rule, which gave continuity to economic policy. In the 1960s, the government introduced tax incentives and loans to encourage mergers and take-overs to help inefficient industries and develop new ones. The post-war French economy prospered up to the early 1970s when growth was retarded. This brought about stop-go policies that further hindered growth and led to a fall in investment and an increase in bankruptcies. The government responded with tax increases, and wage and price restraint, together with attempts to restructure the economy. This led to high unemployment and high inflation.

In the early 1980s, the new socialist government of President Mitterrand increased the legal minimum wage, social benefits and paid holidays, while reducing the working week and offering retirement for all at 60. This caused inflation, increased production costs and led to serious balance of payment problems, resulting in three devaluations. In order to tackle the crisis, in 1983 the socialist government froze prices and wages, tightened exchange controls and increased taxes. The economy started to recover and changes of government saw the implementation of new policies. Oil and finance companies were privatised and rates of personal and corporation taxation were reduced, though social insurance contributions increased – leaving the French one of the most taxed nations in Europe. Nevertheless, the French economy remains one of the strongest in the world.

Types of company

- Société Anonyme (SA) – a corporation which may be quoted or unquoted. Of the top 200 companies, 62 are still actively family controlled, eg. Michelin, Pernod.
- Société à Responsabilité Limitée (SARL) – limited liability companies. These are the most popular type of company in France. Two shareholders are needed.
- Société en Nom Collectif (SNC) – a general partnership. All partners, known as commerçants, have unlimited liability for all the debts and obligations of the partnership.
- Société en Commandite – a limited partnership, by guarantee (société en commandite simple) or with shares (société en commandite par actions). This is not popular.
- Groupement d'Intérêt Economique (GIE) – an economic interest group. They are joint ventures, but with a legal status. They are often used for exports, research and development, etc.
- Enterprise Individuelle – a sole trader with unlimited liability. The sole trader must be registered with the Clerk of the Commercial Court (Tribunal de Commerce).

Banks

Many small banks disappeared in the years after the war, but by the 1980s there was a crisis in the financial system and the banks lost custom and thus profitability. Most of the banking sector was nationalised in 1982, giving the state 90% of loans and credit. The inspiration was both socialist and an attempt to modernise the system, but four categories remain.

- High street and merchant banks.
- Mutualist and co-operatives.
- Sociétés Financières, which specialise in leasing and hire purchase.
- Specialist state controlled institutions such as Crédit National, which provide state credit for industrial investment, department stores, 250 supermarkets and 735 other outlets.

France has five of the nine largest banks in Europe, including the Banque Nationale de Paris and Crédit Lyonnais. There are a substantial number of foreign and regional banks. The Banque de France is the central bank, and it is greatly assisted in its pursuit of monetary policy by the state ownership of such a large section of the banking system.

The Stock Exchange

France has seven stock exchanges, with the modernised Paris Exchange being one of the largest in the world. The privatisation of the 1980s greatly increased the number of French shareholders.

Germany

After the second World War employers and unions worked together to achieve higher output but in recent years attitudes have changed and people are taking life easier. The younger people want to spend more time with their families, to have time to spend their money, and to have more holidays, but they do not want to trade more leisure time for less wages. In addition, the introduction of more machinery and industrial robots in manufacturing plants has alienated many workers.

The reunification of Germany has caused problems in both parts of the country. The old East Germany has found it difficult to adapt. To modernise will be expensive, and this has helped to cause economic problems for the country. At first, reunification boosted the economy, but it then slowed, inflation grew and the balance of payments worsened (though still in surplus). This led to a tight monetary policy, with high interest rates. Economic performance in the East is disappointing, and unemployment relatively high, and public sector spending on the East is large – though the East German economy accounts for only 7% of the national total GNP. Wages are among the highest in the world, and those in the East have almost reached Western levels. Since reunification, growth has slowed and inflation increased. There is little doubt that reunification has cost the West a great deal, but the German economy remains one of the strongest in the world.

Types of company

Handelsgesetz is the strict commercial code within which business activities operate. Many companies employ lawyers to ensure that the rules are not broken.

- Aktiengesellschaft (AG) – corporations, the only type of company whose shares can be traded on the stock exchange. There are about 2,000 of these in Germany.
- Gesellschaft mit beschränkter Haftung (GmbH) – private companies with a limited number of shareholders, and often a family business.
- Offene Handelsgesellschaft (OHG) – a general partnership with unlimited liability.
- Kommanditgesellschaft (KG) – a limited partnership. At least one partner must assume unlimited liability and conduct the company's affairs.
- Gesellschaft des bürgerlichen Rechts (GbR) – a civil law partnership, whose members agree to share specified aspects of their separate business. For example, they may share costs of an office but keep their own earnings.
- Einzelkaufmann – a sole trader, with unlimited liability. The trade name must be registered.

Banks

The Bundesbank is Germany's central bank, responsible for safeguarding the currency. The largest commercial banks are the Deutsche Bank, Dresdner Bank, Commerzbank. They have powerful international reputations. There are also a great many regional and foreign banks. A branch of a bank exists for every 1,370 of the population and there is a bank employee for every 100, which are very high figures.

Banks and companies are closely linked, with representatives often sitting on the supervisory boards of companies. These supervisory boards hire the management boards and approve major financial decisions, so the bank representative provides the financial expertise. Banks also have shares in major companies, so they are secure from takeovers and know they have sound long-term futures.

The Stock Exchange

Germans are considered to be good savers, but not great risk-takers. The stock market is surprisingly small, but growing. Only about 10% of the population are shareholders.

Greece

In the private sector there are a very large number of small, family-run businesses. Greek firms have found export markets hard to penetrate, largely because of this. There are many state-owned public utilities, and although there is talk of privatisation in the future, nothing has yet happened.

Greece is poor and underdeveloped by EU standards, but the country has had stable government since the end of military rule in 1974, and this has allowed a coherent economic policy to be implemented. Greece has suffered balance of payments problems for many years, together with relatively high inflation and low investment in industry.

Government action in the late 1980s has helped stabilise the economy. The devaluation of the Drachma, the introduction of wage controls, exchange controls and import deposits had a real effect. Imports were reduced, and tourism, especially, was encouraged. Large companies that ran into financial trouble in the 1980s have been government-run. Inflation fell, but continues to run at a high figure compared to the rest of Europe. The government has also tried to encourage investment by offering grants and by the rapid issue of permits but a lack of overall confidence in the Greek economy has limited the policy's success. The other way in which Greek government has been able to remain solvent is by borrowing from the EU, and there have been several disputes over the terms of repayment. It is expected that these will be cleared if the government's privatisation programme is effected.

Types of company

- Anonymos Eteria (ARE) – a company limited by shares, similar to a public limited company in the UK
- Eteria Periorismenis Epthinus (EPE) – a limited liability company
- General Partnership (OE) is a partnership with unlimited liability
- Limited Partnership (EE) is a partnership in which at least one member has unlimited liability and at least one other has limited liability
- Maritime Company (NE) exists to allow the ownership, operation or management of Greek or foreign flag merchant vessels
- Sole traders.

Banks

The Bank of Greece is the central bank, and has begun to perform the usual functions of such institutions in the management of the monetary system.

Major commercial banks with branches throughout the country include the Ionian Bank of Greece and the Commercial Bank of Greece. In addition, there are regional and local banks, and specialist banks, such as the Agricultural Bank which will loan to the agricultural sector, and the National Mortgage Bank which assists potential property owners. About 20 foreign banks have branches in Greece. They are the main source of independent financing for overseas investors.

The Stock Exchange

The stock exchange is based in Athens with a branch in Salonika. Share ownership is not common and is largely confined to industries such as shipping.

Ireland

In the 1930s, the Irish government found that it lacked the capital to develop many industries adequately. This led to the development of key industries owned jointly by the state and private shareholders. They became known as semi-state industries, and the concept gained the approval of the trade unions. In recent years, there has been a greater emphasis on acquiring more financial investment from the private sector, so as to ensure that modernisation was possible.

The Industrial Development Authority was founded in the 1950s to encourage overseas investment. By the mid 1960s, the media in Ireland had created an expectation of comparable standards of living with the UK, and to a lesser extent the rest of Europe. For many people, this has been achieved but at the cost of high unemployment for others. The professions have prospered, often through tax concessions. Indeed, it is only recently that farmers paid tax. There has always been a large group of poor in Ireland and they have remained in that position while the rest of the country has prospered. Tight fiscal control under Prime Minister Garret Fitzgerald in the early 1980s began to gain some control of the economy. He was replaced by Charles Haughey, who undertook a policy of cuts in public expenditure, with the eventual result that the Punt is strong, and inflation has fallen though unemployment remains high.

Foreign investment is encouraged, and capital has come from the UK, Germany, the USA, Japan, France, and the Netherlands. Tourism has helped the economy. Ireland has also been able to attract overseas visitors with holiday homes.

Types of company

The company structure is similar to that of the UK.

Banks

The Central Bank of Ireland is the main monetary authority. It is independent of government, but lays down reserve requirements for the other banks, acts as their banker, ensures compliance with the European Monetary System requirements, and operates an exchange for the clearance of cheques. It manages the accounts of the government and is the custodian of official reserves. Commercial banking is dominated by two Irish groups, the Bank of Ireland and Allied Irish Banks. Others include Ulster Bank, owned by the National Westminster Bank, and the National Irish Bank, owned by the National Australia Bank. There are a large number of foreign banks operating in Ireland.

The main state lending institutions include the Industrial Credit Corporation, which provides medium and long term capital for industry, and the Agricultural Credit corporation which lends to agriculture and the agro-industry.

The Stock Exchange

The Stock Exchange deals mainly in government stocks. Shares in Irish Companies, such as Guinness, trade mainly in the UK. The actual trading floor of the Dublin Stock Exchange is small, and share dealings are not important in Irish society.

Italy

Features of the Italian economy include the large size of state sector, the large number of family firms and the large number of small firms. This suggests a mixture of politics, social values and competition. Two important government companies offer links between the public and private sectors. Instituto per la Ricostruzione Industriale (IRI) was established by the government in 1933 to tackle bankruptcies. Its role evolved and it is now the largest service and investment company in Europe. Ente Nazionale Idrocarburi (ENI) was established in 1953 to dispose of the assets of the Agenzia Generale Italiana Petrolferi. It expanded into oil exploration, drilling and petrochemicals. These are the major state holding companies, which are overseen by the Ministero per le Partecipazioni Statali, the Ministry of State Holdings, which is responsible to Parliament.

There are also government-controlled boards (enti), whose capital is provided by the state, and who have a controlling interest in many firms. As private shareholding is fragmented, the state can often have control with less than 25% of the equity capital. State corporations control 80% of Italy's banking, 25% of industrial employment and 50% of fixed investment. The Italian nationalised industries are wholly state financed so that there are public and semi-public bodies.

By the end of the 1970s, as a result of terrorism, political unrest and industrial weakness, the country faced a crisis. Moreover, the public sector became a major drain on the country's resources. A decade later, reconstruction of the manufacturing centre had caused much unemployment, but the trade unions had co-operated and the economy had performed well. However, in the 1990s, difficulties began to emerge, largely as a result of the large public sector deficit. The collapse of the state holding company EFIM in 1992 seriously dented confidence, and there is a general feeling that the others should be dispersed. Moreover, unemployment is high, especially in the south, and interest rates are among the highest in Europe. Labour costs have risen sharply, and inflation is relatively high, so the country is in an extremely difficult position.

Types of company

- Società per Azioni (SpA) – a public limited company.
- Società a Responsabilita Limitata (Srl) – a private limited company.
- Società in Nome Collettivo – unlimited liability partnership.
- Società in Accomandita Semplice (Sas) – limited liability partnership.
- Società in Accomandita Azioni (SapA) – liability of some partners unlimited.

All businesses must be registered with the local Chamber of Commerce (Camera del Commercio).

Banks

There are 1,200 separate banks in Italy, with about 12,000 branches. Thus the system is scattered and uncompetitive. Many of the banks are state-owned and jobs are often given as a political reward. Banking services are poor, and are characterised by long queues. Recently a nationwide cash dispenser system was introduced. The cards were supposed to be usable in all banks, but this did not happen. Computers have been introduced but this has not resulted in any reduction of staff.

The Banca d'Italia (Bank of Italy) is the central bank. It is state-owned, but maintains an independence. The Governor is appointed for life, which provides security and continuity. Recent amalgamations have created about half a dozen major commercial banks, including Banca Nazionale del Lavoro, Credito Italiano and Banca Commerciale Italiana. Many banks are small local savings banks (Casse di Risparmio) which receive funds from local investors and lend to local firms, thus preserving local identity and sound working relationships and using local knowledge for decisions.

The Stock Exchange

The Milan Stock Market has only about 200 quoted companies, with active trading in only about 50. Italy has no anti-trust legislation, no monopolies and mergers commission and no insider trading laws. Thus, the Milan Stock exchange is not appealing to investors.

Luxembourg

Luxembourg is a very prosperous country with a high standard of living. The economy centres around two main industries – banking and steel. The steel crisis of the 1970s forced a reduction in output and manpower. Luxembourg needs to import all of its energy needs, and the rising price of oil worsened the situation and led to deficits on the visible trade balance. This increased the importance to the economy of agriculture, banking and tourism. The financial sector in particular has greatly helped the balance of payments. The steel industry has emerged as a smaller but more efficient producer, and continues to make a major contribution to the wealth of the nation. At the same time, however, there is strong international pressure for Luxembourg to relax its strict laws on banking secrecy. This has spurred the government to attempt to diversify its industries by attracting foreign, highly tech-nological, manufacturers to Luxembourg. These include US firms such as General Motors and Goodyear.

Types of company

Their law recognises the following trading companies.

- Enterprise Individuelle – sole trader.
- Société en nom collectif (Senc) – partnership.
- Société en commandite simple (Secs) – limited partnership.
- Société anonyme (SA) – public limited company.
- Société en commandite par actions (Seca) – partnership limited by shares.
- Société à responsabilité limitée (Sarl) – limited liability company.
- Société co-operative (SC) – co-operative.

Every commercial and industrial enterprise must obtain a government licence to trade. Individuals must demonstrate qualifications and good character; for partnerships and companies this applies to the individual responsible for the management.

Banks

There is no central bank but the centre of the financial community is Banque et Caisse d'Epargne de l'Etat, Luxembourg (The State and Savings Bank, Luxembourg). This is an independent public establishment, but the capital belongs to the state and it holds government funds. Société Nationale de Crédit et d'Investissement (SNCI) is a state funded autonomous public institution created in 1977 to stimulate the country's economy by loans and credits to firms. The co-operative and agricultural savings institutions are small, and lend to small businesses and agricultural concerns. The number of commercial banks in Luxembourg has grown greatly in recent years, with many foreign banks setting up branches in the country. Much of their work involves transactions in the security business conducted in Luxembourg.

Apart from commercial banking operations, Luxembourg is the home of the credit and investment department of the European Union and of the European Investment Bank which raises large sums for capital projects within the EU and associated countries. The main domestic banks are Banque Internationale à Luxembourg, Banque Générale du Luxembourg, Kredietbank SA and Caisse d'Epargne de l'Etat.

The system is supervised by the Luxembourg Monetary Institute which has a Council of seven government nominees to guide the general policy of the Institute and an Executive Committee of a Director General and two Directors.

The Stock Exchange

Transactions are in cash only. Much of the trade is in the rapidly expanding securities market.

Netherlands

There is a close relationship between the government, employers and workers. This began after the war, when the first post-war governments were socialist, and declared that the national economy could prosper only with a social, economic and financial programme.

Dutch industry is dominated by four multi-nationals – Philips, Unilever, Royal Dutch Shell and Akzo. Unilever is 50% UK-owned and Shell 40%. In the 1970s and 1980s they were involved in considerable overseas investment, starving the domestic industries of capital. However, money has come from overseas, largely because of the Commissariaat voor de Buitenlandsa Investeringen (CBIN) – the Commissariat for Foreign Investment – which worked hard to attract such capital.

The largest reserves of gas in Europe was discovered in the northern province of Groningen in 1959. This greatly assisted industrialisation in the 1960s and 1970s, but much money was spent on private and public consumption rather than investment. The oil was exported, giving a balance of trade surplus, forcing up the value of the Guilder, and making other exports uncompetitive. High public spending and high wage demands were both hidden by the gas revenue. The slump from the 1970s in oil and gas prices reduced revenue, and so helped the decline of the economy. There is now a policy of energy conservation which in the 1980s, together with deregulation and privatisation, helped lower public spending, coupled with reductions in the public sector workforce. However, unemployment rose, increasing social welfare payments and bringing about further cuts in public spending.

The Netherlands appears prosperous, but the problems of unemployment and a huge budget deficit remain. Taxation and national insurance payments are very high. The strong technological base of the country provides hope that there is sufficient economic strength to overcome the difficulties.

Types of company

- Bestolen Vennootschap met beperkte aansprakelijkheid (BV) – a private company with limited liability.
- Naamloze Vennootschap (NV) – a public company.
- Vennootschap onder Firma (FOV) – an unlimited partnership.
- Commanditaire Vennootschap (CV) – a partnership with both limited and unlimited partners.
- Co-operative Vereniging – a co-operative. Every co-operative must give an indication of its objectives and initials to indicate the liability of its members: WA (unlimited), BA (limited), and UJA (no liability).
- Eenmanszaak – a sole trader
- Overheidsbedrijven – state-controlled enterprise.

All partnerships must be recorded in the Trade Register.

Every new business must register with the local offices of direct taxation, indirect taxation and social security, and must be entered in the Handels-register (trade register) of the district in which the head office is located. It is kept at the municipal or regional office of the Chamber of Commerce, of which all companies are members, and have to pay an annual fee. The Public Nuisance Act demands that any business that could cause a danger, damage, or nuisance must have a licence.

Banks

The central bank is the Nederlandsche Bank which, in conjunction with the Minister of Finance, controls monetary policy. The 1948 Bank Act gave three tasks to the Bank: currency regulation, note and coin issue and credit facilities. There are four main commercial banks – Rabobank, ABN (Algemene Bank Nederland), Amrobank, Nederlandsche Middenstands-bank (NMB) which offer a wide range of facilities. Postbank (National Giro) is very important for personal accounts, and is used by almost half the population. Hypotheekbanken deal in long-term mortgage loans for industrial or domestic purposes. Spaarbanken are savings banks. The

Nationale Investeringsbank, jointly owned by the government and other banks, gives long-term loans. The Maatschappij Industriele Projecten (Company for Industrial Projects) is a consortium of government, banks and institutional investors with venture capital, especially for high technology.

The Stock market

The only stock exchange is located at Amsterdam and is the oldest in the world.

Norway

After the Second World War, Norway concentrated on heavy engineering industries such as shipbuilding. These began to decline in the mid-1970s but Norway was able to sustain its economic prosperity with a strong energy sector. Hydro-electric power reduced overheads for larger industries such as aluminium. Moreover, Norway became a major oil exporter. In recent years, there has been a depression in manufacturing and an increase in the service sector and the public sector. High public spending, based on oil revenues, pushed up wages and helped slow the rise in unemployment, but inhibited growth in the private sector. There was a severe recession from 1986 to 1991, with some recovery in 1992 and 1993. In 1993, interest rates fell, which boosted private consumption.

Norway has a highly developed social welfare programme, so the relatively high unemployment has increased government spending considerably and caused difficulties with the budget. Although inflation is fairly low, this is a problem that could take time to solve. Recently, however, modest wage settlements have made Norwegian wage costs less unattractive but Norway remains vulnerable to changes in oil prices.

Types of company

- Joint stock company.
- Partnership (general or limited).
- Sole trader.

Banks

The central bank is Norges Bank, which advises the Ministry of Finance on credit and monetary policy, and is responsible for its implementation. The three largest commercial banks are Den Norske Bank (DNB), Kreditkassen (known abroad as Christiania Bank) and the Fokus Bank, which are all state owned.

The credit market is both public and private. The public sector includes the Post Giro, Post Office Savings Bank, and the other state banks such as the State Housing Bank. The private sector includes the commercial banks, savings banks, loan associations, mortgage companies and insurance companies. The distinction between the sectors has blurred in recent years. Several of the commercial and savings banks found themselves in difficulties in the late 1980s because of a slump in the property market, lax lending policies and the recession. To combat this, the Government Bank Insurance Fund was established in 1991 to help stabilise institutions in difficulty. The three largest commercial banks became state-owned as a result of this rescue operation, but the government intends to privatise them in the future.

The Stock Exchange

The most important activity on the Oslo Stock Exchange is trade in equities and bonds.

Portugal

The dictator Salazar was toppled in 1974, after which a stable constitutional democracy emerged. However, the country remained heavily dependent on agriculture. Before joining the European Union in 1986, Portugal had a stagnant economy. However, assisted by EU transfers and foreign invest- ment, industry has developed, the economy has grown, and inflation has fallen, although it remains high by the standards of western Europe. There is a consistent trade deficit, which is at least partially countered by invisibles and in particular tourism and money sent back to Portugal by emigrant workers. The government began to privatise the businesses nationalised in 1974, and is seeking foreign investors to develop industry. At the moment, Portugal is troubled by high inflation, an inefficient and large agricultural sector, and a disparity between the more prosperous north and the poorer south.

The public sector is extensive and includes banking, insurance, steel, public transport, electricity, gas and water supply, sanitation, harbours and airports, shipbuilding, armaments, beer and petrochemicals. A privatisa- tion programme was begun in 1989 and will continue slowly.

Types of company

- Estabelecimento Individual – sole trader with unlimited liability.
- Estabelecimento Individual de Responsabilidade Limitade (EIRL) – sole trader with limited liability.
- Sociedade em Comandita (SC) – partnership where sleeping partners have unlimited liability and active or full partners are fully liable.
- Sociedade em Nome olectio – limited partnership.
- Sociedade por Quotas (Lda) – private limited company.
- Sociedade Anonima (SA) – public limited company.

Banks

The central bank is the Bank of Portugal. The National Development Bank (Banco de Fomento) grants medium- and long-term credits for the nation's economic development. There are commercial banks, but they are mainly nationalised.

The Stock Exchange

The Lisbon Stock Exchange is one of the oldest in the world. The Oporto Stock Exchange was founded in 1891. The main dealings are in bonds and equities.

Spain

Until the death of Franco in 1975, Spain was isolated from the rest of Europe and had many small companies, inadequate training, poor public services and infrastructure and ETA terrorism. Stable government emerged after an uneasy transition, and a programme of economic reconstruction was begun in 1984. Spain joined the EU on 1 January 1986, and in the first two years afterwards 150,000 small businesses failed as a result of foreign competition. The reductions in tariff barriers saw an influx of goods and a deterioration in the balance of payments, but exports have begun to increase.

The reconstruction programme began to have some success, with the state holding company for heavy industry, INI, making its first profit since 1975 in 1988. It now accounts for more than 30% of Spanish production. The government has also encouraged the growth of new technology through its National Electronics and Information Technology plan. After 1987 as a result of the government's special employment programmes and tax incentives to industry to create new jobs, investment in plant and machinery has grown, and the inflow of foreign capital has continued. 1988 and 1989 were boom years, with growth, increases in exports, and high investment. This continued at a more moderate level in 1990.

Opposition to a youth employment programme to create jobs on minimum wages from the trade unions led to a general strike on 14 January 1988. Further strikes showed opposition to reductions in unemployment benefits. The breakdown in relations with the unions is serious, especially as steady consumer demand and relatively low inflation needs to continue, and wage restraint would help this.

In 1989, the government introduced a Regional Development Plan, a public investment programme to develop the infrastructure, especially the roads. In addition, the regions have their own development plans, many of which attract EU finding. The regions can levy taxes, eg. wealth tax and surcharges on government income tax.

Types of company

The legal framework was established in the years of Franco. There was no obligation for firms to undergo independent audits, and only recently have many firms been persuaded that this could be of value to them. All businesses except sole traders have to register in the Mercantile Register of the provincial capital in which the firm's head office is located.

- Sociedad Anonima (SA) can be public or private, large or small. The capital requirement for compulsory registration has been reduced from 50m Pesetas to 3m.
- Sociedad de Responsabilidad Limitada (SRL/SL) requires no minimum capital and is stock exchange quoted with some restrictions on the transfer of shares, but few other requirements.
- Sociedades Colectivas – partnerships, which are uncommon in Spain, and have unlimited liability.
- Sociedad Comanditaria/en Comandita – limited partnership, with at least one limited and one unlimited pattern.
- Co-operativas – co-operatives. All co-operatives must enter the Co-operative Register. The most famous co-operative, Mondragon, in the Basques, was founded in 1956. It has over 100 enterprises, employs 20,000 people, has its own bank, social security system, and even its own technical college. It has attracted world-wide attention.
- Comerciante – a sole trader, who is automatically a member of the local chamber of commerce.
- Joint Ventures – either temporary or permanent among firms with financial incentives.

Banks

The Banco de España is the central bank and was nationalised in 1962. In the 1970s it began to manage monetary policy and now also supervises the banking system. It is responsible to the Ministry of Economy and Finance. It has helped fight inflation, and has high currency reserves. Private banks are national, regional and local. There are well over 100 in total, but the top six control 75% of the market. These are the Banco Bilbao Vizcaya (BBV), Banco Central, Banco Español de Credito (Banesto), Banco Hispano Americano, Banco de Santander and Banco Popular. There are also about 40 foreign banks operating in Spain, and these tend to lend to the largest companies. Cajas de Ahorros (savings banks) are similar to building societies in the UK. They have no shareholders and are non-profit making. The biggest, La Caixa (Barcelona) and Caja Madris are as large as the second the third banks in Spain. Co-operatives de Credito (co-operative savings banks) include the rural banks, whose members are agricultural cooperatives and general co-operatives. Their assets are small.

The Instituo de Credito Official (ICO) co-ordinates and directs the official credit institutions, and provides most of the funding. The institutions are publicly owned limited liability companies that act on behalf of the monetary authorities to complement private initiatives. They are Banco de Credito Agricola, Banco Hipotecario de España, Banco de Credito Industrial and Banco de Credito Local. Each deals in a specific area, namely agriculture, housing, manufacturing industry and local authorities. State loans provide the funding, together with loans from the capital and interbank money markets.

The Stock Market

The Stock Market is old fashioned and not very active. 80% of transactions take place in Madrid, 15% at Barcelona, and 5% between Bilbao and Valencia. There has been more domestic interest in shares recently. Foreigners can invest, but need special permission to acquire more than 50% of a company's stock.

Sweden

Most of Sweden's industries are privately owned, but there is state ownership in mining, the utilities, transport and communications. Sweden is an advanced industrial national with one of the highest standards of social welfare in the world. Its has industries associated with forestry, heavy engineering, textiles and vehicles. When the recession hit the steel, ship building and textile industries in the 1970s there was restructuring by the state but these were sold off in the 1980s. The 1980s demonstrated that the government had acted wisely, and the economy continued to prosper, but the general recession of the 1990s saw a fall in GDP, and a serious fall in investment. High interest rates and falling property prices have assisted the trend. The budget deficit is growing, and the reduced production and higher unemployment provided a smaller tax base to support higher unemployment benefits. Government policy aims to retain full employment, that is 2–3% unemployment, while controlling inflation, but this has not been achieved, and the Swedish economy is under considerable pressure.

Types of company

- Aktiebolag (AB) – a limited liability company, and the most common form of company in Sweden.
- Handelsbolag – an unlimited partnership, recorded on the trade register.
- Kommanditbolag – a limited partnership.
- Filial till utlandskt bolag – a branch of a foreign corporation.
- Enskild firma – a sole trader.

Banks

The central bank, the Riksbanken, was founded in 1668 and is the oldest central bank in the world. It is supervised by the Swedish Parliament. The chairman of its board of governors is a government appointee. The Bank and the government work together to co-ordinate economic policy. It also issues notes and administers the foreign exchange reserves. Sweden has three groups of banks:

- Commercial Banks have 62% of total bank deposits. Four banks have over 80% of the assets, and are represented throughout the country – Skandinaviska Enskilda Banken, Svenska Handelsbanken, Nordbanken and Gota Bank.
- Savings Banks have 30% of deposits. Mergers have reduced the number of savings banks so that just over 100 remain.
- Co-operative Banks have 8% deposits. There are about 400 co-operative banks. These are local, and originally existed to offer banking services to farmers, but are now available to all customers. Heavy losses in 1990/92 caused them to seek government assistance, and in October 1992, the government provided a guarantee to depositors to maintain the stability of the co-operative banks. The distinctions between the three are becoming increasingly blurred.

The government appoints directors to the central, regional and local boards of the banks, and approves the appointment of each chairman. There is a Finance Inspection Board which supervises banks and insurance companies. There are also about 100 finance houses, many owned by the banks.

The Stock Exchange

The Stockholm Stock Exchange has the exclusive right to deal in public offerings and securities.

Switzerland

The Swiss economy is founded on the principle of non-intervention by the state, whose role is to create conditions favourable to the development of private enterprise. Switzerland has one of the highest GNPs per head in the world. It is a highly industrialised country. The lack of raw materials made trade essential from the onset, to finance imports of materials. It is dominated by large companies such as Schindler, Georg Fischer, Landis und Gyr, SIG. It is the home of multi-nationals such as Nestlé, Hoffman-La Roche, Ciba-Geigy, Sandoz. Swiss industry is always technologically advanced. There was a steady growth in the 1980s, but overheating in 1988 brought on a recession, as the Swiss National Bank was slow to impose monetary measures. The recession led to a realisation that the economic framework needed restructuring. The cartels, price control and protectionism came under scrutiny and legislation is likely.

Inflation is normally very low, at 2–4% per annum, although in the early 1990s it did reach 6% before falling. In the same way, unemployment has been almost non-existent, but the recent recession pushed the Swiss figure to almost 5% in 1994/95. This is about half the average figure for the European Union, but very high by Swiss standards.

Types of Company

- Sole trader.
- Partnership.
- Limited partnership.
- Partnership limited by shares.
- Public limited company, which is the most popular form of business in Switzerland.
- Limited liability company.
- Co-operative.

All types of business unit must be recorded on the Register of Commerce.

Banks

The central bank is the Swiss National Bank. 59% of its share capital is held by the cantons and 41% by private shareholders. It is responsible for implementing monetary policy. There are almost 600 banks in Switzerland, of which just over one-third are foreign-owned. They account for 8% of GDP. They fall into three categories. Many of the banks are private, and relatively little is known of their actual size because they are not legally obliged to provide full details of all the funds that they manage. They concentrate on portfolio management. Three large banks have branches throughout the country, and dominate the national market. These are the Union Bank of Switzerland, Swiss Bank Corporation and Crédit Suisse. Each canton has its own bank, which operates only within the cantonal boundaries. In addition, there are local commercial and savings banks operating within an even more restricted radius. The Federal Banking Commission supervises the banking sector and mutual funds.

The Stock Exchange

In 1990 there were seven, but now there are only three. Major business is transacted on the Zurich Exchange.

Insurance

A number of Europe's most powerful insurance companies are based in Switzerland, and there is also a significant Swiss presence in reinsurance, including Swiss Re which is the second largest firm of its type in Europe. The Swiss themselves tend to be heavily insured.

United Kingdom

The recession of the early 1980s brought about a drastic decline to the nation's manufacturing base. This caused unemployment. The government's response was a tight monetary policy, with high interest rates and reduced spending, which was unpopular with everyone, including business itself, though it did help to reduce inflation. At the same time, the policies of competition and free enterprise, with reduced state intervention and privatisation were introduced. By 1990, 42% of 1979s nationalised industries had been transferred to the private sector, including gas and electricity, water and the telephone system.

Central government began to control the spending of local authorities, and so was able to exert some influence over the nature of local government expenditure. Government policies reduced the number of strikes, and improved industrial productivity, but at the cost of high unemployment and low economic growth. The balance of trade has also been in deficit. The sale of state assets and the revenue from North Sea oil was used to support the growing numbers of unemployed, rather than to try to revitalise industry and has now been spent.

On the other hand, foreign investment in the UK has grown rapidly in recent years. In 1986, foreign companies invested £4.8b in the UK; in 1987 £8.1b; in 1988 £7.1b. Much of this has come from Japan as the UK has failed to attract significant investment from other countries. The first Japanese company invested in the UK in 1972 and by 1989 there were about 100. Japanese investors are interested in the prospects of the European market, and wish to avoid any possible external tariffs. The UK is attractive because the Japanese learn English as a compulsory subject at school, so language is not a major barrier, as it would be in any other European country; corporation taxes are relatively low; there is a sound distribution system; ease of access to the rest of Europe, especially with the opening of the Channel tunnel; improved labour relations and competitive wage rates.

Types of company

The main types of business organization in the private sector are:

- Sole traders.
- Partnerships.

- Private limited companies.
- Public limited companies (PLCs) whose shares are quoted on the Stock Exchange.
- Cooperatives.

Banks

The Bank of England was founded in 1694, and nationalised in 1946. This is the central bank of the UK, and is responsible for issue of notes and coins, the management of the national debt, and acts as the banker of the government and the other banks, controls foreign reserves, and implements the nation's monetary policy. All other banks operating in the UK are subject to the supervision and regulation of the Bank of England.

Domestic banking in England and Wales is dominated by the four largest banks – Barclays, Lloyds, Midland and National Westminster, all of which have branches throughout the country, and so can offer financial services to all UK businesses. In recent years, business customers have increasingly looked to the banks to provide working capital as well as money to finance expansion. However, the banks have alienated customers (both personal and small business) as well as shareholders. All of the Big Four have written off large debts which have resulted from loans to Third World countries, and have tried to recoup some of this loss by imposing greater charges on customers.

The number of building societies has fallen as a result of mergers. Three of the largest are the Halifax, Nationwide Anglia and the Woolwich. The main function of building societies is to loan money to individuals to purchase their own homes and this accounts for about 80% of the combined funds of the societies. Building Societies are now able to do more than just loan money for house purchase, and so they offer personal loans, cheque books and credit cards, and in many ways act like commercial banks. There is increasing competition between the two and the distinction between them is starting to disappear. Indeed, the second largest building society, the Abbey National, became a bank in 1989.

The Stock Market

The Conservative Government of the 1980s has encouraged the simplification of the Stock Exchange, so as to make transactions easier and cheaper. This led to mergers and takeovers, as the banks and other financial institutions began to offer stock exchange services for customers.

Activity

- □ The students should consider the commercial and economic base of their chosen European country.
- □ Looking at the type of material contained within the chapter, the students should decide on the information they require.
- □ They should decide what sources they should consult in order to compile the information.
- □ The information should be gathered and presented to their contemporaries. They should indicate their sources, and explain any difficulties that they have encountered.
- □ It may be difficult to obtain this information and so the students could require more assistance at the preparation stage.
- □ This could be the basis for another assessment, as it offers the students an opportunity to develop research skills, but with material that can be found relatively easily. Nevertheless, it provides a greater degree of difficulty than Activity 1.

Chapter Six

The Workforce

Aims of this chapter

☐ To show the different educational systems which operate and demonstrate the various approaches to training in Western Europe
☐ To determine the qualifications and organization of the workforce, and investigate the possible relationship between these and the strength of the industrial base of each country
☐ To examine where appropriate the impact of immigrant labour
☐ To explore the law relating to the employer/employee relationships and discuss the size and strength of the trade union movements
☐ To consider the relative prosperity of each country.

GDP (Gross Domestic Product) measures the value of goods and services generated by an economy during a given period – usually twelve months.

Such figures are, however, virtually meaningless unless related to population size and expressed in a common unit of measurement. Even so, this may tell us little about comparative levels of prosperity.

Purchasing Power Standards (PPS) indicate the volume of goods and services which a given sum of money will buy. If this is linked to expenditure on social benefits and to ownership of consumer durables, then prosperity and living standards can be compared in a simple yet reasonably accurate way.

STANDARD OF LIVING

INTERNATIONAL COMPARISON

Countries	GDP at Market Prices	Social Benefits	Passenger Cars	Televisions	Telephones
	1991	1991	1990	1990	1991
	per inhabitants in PPS*		per 1000 inhabitants		
Luxembourg	19636	5797	477	255	498
Germany (FR)	18345	4952	481	—	526
Belgium	16193	4191	387	452	—
France	17250	4803	414	406	—
Italy	15890	3991	456	424	—
Netherlands	15551	5101	367	495	—
Denmark	16576	4609	309	535	577
Ireland	10815	2240	226	276	292
United Kingdom	14732	3654	374	435	—
Greece	7397	1669	172	196	414
Portugal	9064	1617	259	177	—
Spain	11964	2433	308	394	—

* Purchasing Power standards

Source: Service central de la statistique et des études Economiques, Luxembourgh

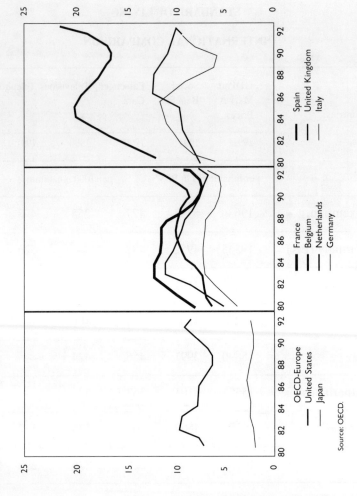

CHART 3 – UNEMPLOYMENT RATE
(Percentages of the labour force)

Source: OECD.

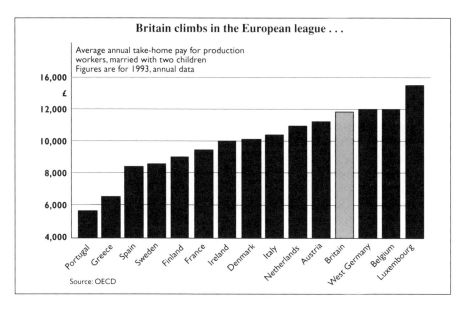

Britain climbs in the European league . . .

Average annual take-home pay for production
workers, married with two children
Figures are for 1993, annual data

Source: OECD

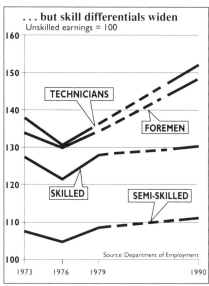

. . . but skill differentials widen

Unskilled earnings = 100

TECHNICIANS

FOREMEN

SKILLED

SEMI-SKILLED

Source: Department of Employment

1973   1976   1979   1990

Austria

Education and training

Crèches, day care centres and kindergartens are available for all children, but compulsory education begins at the age of six and lasts for nine years. Four years are spent at primary school and then there is a choice: four years of basic secondary education followed by a one year polytechnic course leading to employment, or eight years of general secondary education which results in a school leaving certificate and allows university entry. It is possible to switch between the two systems.

For students aged between 14 and 19, there is a wide range of vocational options available. Certain occupations can be learnt only at school, such as medicine, teaching and engineering. Others, such as paper hanging or floristry, can only be undertaken by the dual vocational system which combines training apprentices in workshops and vocational schools. Apprentices are obliged to attend the vocational schools.

There are two universities and six colleges of art in Austria offering a wide range of academic courses. About 16% of those born in a given year attend university. In addition, there are 350 adult education colleges and 2,400 local institutes. About 10% of the Austrian population attend individual lectures each year, and about 250,000 attend regular courses, mostly further vocational training.

Trade unions

Employment is established by a contract and, once agreed, becomes subject to the labour laws. There is an Agreement Law, which covers agreements. Labour laws relate to hours, holidays and dismissal. The usual working week is up to 40 hours, and paid holidays range from 30–36 days, plus public holidays. The 16 individual trade unions in Austria are joined together by the Austrian Federation of Trade Unions, which negotiates with employers over wages and conditions. The tenor is moderate, and disputes are rare. Workers can also discuss employment matters with their employers through elected representatives.

Belgium

Education and training

The Constitution specifies three responsibilities of the central government in relation to education – the period of compulsory education, minimum conditions for the award of diplomas and the pension system – and each of the three communities organise their own education system. The state insists that children will begin compulsory education in the year they attain the age of six, and will receive education for twelve years. After the age of 16, that education may be part-time.

Provision within the communities does vary, but each offers nursery schools for infants, and then primary schools for children aged six to 12 and secondary schools for the 12–18 age group. There are schools and colleges for those who leave school at 16 to receive vocational training to accompany their employment. Higher education is available either in institutions devoted to particular vocational areas, or through the more traditional academic university route. Schools are available for adult education. These are largely, but not exclusively, vocational and include courses for the self-employed.

Trade unions

Unemployment stands at around 8.5%, mainly unskilled workers, with shortages of technicians and some professionals. Belgian employment legislation is extensive. There is a general requirement to provide lengthy notice of termination of employment, regardless of reason, with payment in lieu if notice is inadequate. Employee representation in the workplace and collective bargaining are well-developed. Firms are legally obliged to establish a system of consultation with the workforce. Most companies pay an annual trade union premium to the unions represented within the company to ensure industrial peace. Collective agreements are legally binding. There are few industrial disputes. Belgian labour leaders are considered relatively moderate, and represent both political and religious traditions, while the employers are prepared to compromise.

Denmark

Education and training

In Denmark education is compulsory for children aged between seven and 16, but most stay on after that age. About two thirds attend vocational upper secondary education, which offers three year courses leading to the higher commercial examination and the higher technical examination. The courses alternate periods in industry with time spent in the classroom, so as to marry practice to theory. Local trade committees, which have representatives of employers and employees organizations, are responsible for the individual courses.

About one-third undertake general upper secondary education, which involves three years of study to gain the "Gymnasium" and university entrance. There is provision for older people to return to education, full or part time, to gain a similar award, the HF. Universities offer the more traditional academic courses, and institutions of higher education at university level offer specialised vocational courses and research, such as engineering, pharmacy, business, architecture, etc. In 1990, 954,000 people were receiving education. Of these, 655,000 were under 16, 169,000 were undertaking vocational education and 130,000 were in universities and colleges.

Trade unions

Working conditions are laid down in detailed legislation. About 90% of workers are in unions, which are industry based, eg. Union of Commercial and Clerical Workers, Union of Metal Workers. They are all affiliated to the Danish Confederation of Trade Unions. Danish unions are amongst the most moderate in Europe. Most employers are represented by the Danish Employers Association.

Finland

Education and training

Primary education is compulsory between the ages of seven to 13 and comprehensive schools take care of the needs of the 13 to 16 year olds. There is particular emphasis placed on languages. About one half of school leavers continue at an upper secondary school, which involves three years of study to gain university entrance. About one-third of school leavers attend vocational schools, which are separate institutions for each subject area. Students are either directly from comprehensives or from upper secondary schools. Courses last from two to six years, depending on the level and the subject, and include periods in industry. Apprenticeships are not common in Finland. Practical training and work experience is preferred. Universities offer the more traditional academic courses, and the old vocational institutions are being reorganised into polytechnics to prepare students to work in trade and industry and for management. They are more practical and professionally orientated than the universities.

Adult education is available throughout the country. Courses are available at the vocational colleges, but much work-related education occurs at the place of employment. There is training for the unemployed.

Trade unions

Employers and employees are required to co-operate to maintain and improve safety at work, and the larger firms have committees with representatives from both sides. There is also extensive legislation regarding working conditions and social benefits. Collective bargaining takes place annually between the employers' associations and the trade unions to reach agreement on wages and conditions. The unions are moderate in their approach and disputes are rare.

France

Education and training

Any student with a baccalaureate (a broad based qualification for 18 year olds) is entitled to enter a university. There are also about 175 Grandes Ecoles which provide education in technical, administrative and business areas and admission is competitive and fierce. Large companies recruit from the Grandes Ecoles and some 80% of senior managers in large companies will have attended. About 15,000 a year graduate from the engineering schools, and 8,000 from business schools.

State industry, private firms and civil service all recruit from the same pools, so top managers know each other. Moreover, Treasury officials will move into banking and industry, and back to the state, so contact with government and business is close. Recently, youth schemes have been created, as unemployment in the 16–25 age group is very high (1990, almost one-quarter, three times the German figure, and higher than the UK). The community work contracts (Travaux d'Utilité Collective), and social security relief for employers taking on young people have not been very effective. There are fewer apprenticeships than in Germany, and there is a shortage of skilled workers, engineers and technicians.

Immigrant labour

Immigrants make up nearly 10% of the population of France, with a large group from Moslem North Africa – 780,000 from Algeria, 520,000 from Morocco, and 210,000 from Tunisia and many more from the rest of Europe – 860,000 from Portugal, 425,000 from Italy and 380,000 from Spain. Many came without their families, hoping to save enough to return home to start their own businesses, but most stayed and were joined by their families. They are mainly unskilled, working on building sites, assembly lines and performing unpleasant jobs such as garbage removal. Over three-quarters of immigrants have residence and ten year work permits which are automatically renewable. Racial friction is not uncommon.

Trade unions

The three largest confederations are: Confédération Générale du Travail (CGT), founded in 1895 and strong in state owned sectors such as the utilities and the railways. Its leaders have been members of the Communist

Party. The Confédération Française Démocratique du Travail (CFDT) has a socialist ethos, and is committed to workers' control. Force Ouvrière (FO) is the most moderate, believing in negotiation rather than conflict.

All firms can have union members, and if an employee notifies the head of the firm, he must meet the unions at least twice a year. Employers cannot insist on single-union agreements nor can unions insist on a "closed shop". In all firms, the unions nominate a shop steward (Délégué syndical) who will negotiate with employers, and in companies employing more than ten people the workers elect a délégué du personnel, who solves individual problems but does not negotiate. Each firm which has more than 50 employees must have a works' committee (comité d'enterprise) which must be consulted on health and safety matters, hours of work, wages and redundancies.

All of the union representatives are protected by law. They are allowed time to conduct their union business, and have job protection. In 1982, new laws (les lois Auroux) allowed "expression groups" greater consultation at shop floor level. Workers and management could talk without official union representation. They have been compared to quality circles, which are widespread, and both are disliked by the unions, especially the CGT. Many collective agreements are made on an industrial sector or local basis.

Germany

Education and training

Vocational training centres around the Dual System of three year apprenticeships, with in-company training and vocational schools (Berufsschulen). In 1988, about 1.75 million were undergoing this training. The state runs the vocational schools, and the Chamber of Industry and Commerce (Industrie und Handelskammern) and the Craft Chambers (Handwerkerkammern) inspect the half million approved training firms. Apprentices are registered, supervised and examined by the Chambers. There is a low drop out rate, at around 5%, and 90% pass at the first attempt. They become qualified skilled workers (Facharbeiter), which gives better pay, and the ability to seek higher vocational awards. After a minimum of two years experience, they can undertake higher vocational training (Fortbildung) which allows career progression into supervisory and management positions. About 17,500 a year pass. These higher vocational awards and graduates make up the junior management levels. Most managers are graduates who have taken a career-orientated subject.

In the 1960s, about 100 polytechnics were established to offer three or four year courses that were more vocational and shorter than those of the universities. About a quarter of a million students attend polytechnics, while a million more than this were at universities in the late 1980s. The most popular subjects, in order, are mechanical and production engineering, economics and business, and social studies. There are 68 universities with courses lasting about six years. Polytechnic courses are more practical and less theoretical, so that university graduates have a two year "apprenticeship" after graduation, and often go to large companies, whereas polytechnic graduates go to medium-sized firms, which seldom have induction training.

The most ambitious prospective businessman would take a doctorate in a relevant subject. In 1985, over one-third of management board members of AGs, two-fifths of quoted AGs, and over one-half of management boards of top 100 companies had doctorates.

Firms are committed to management development. Large ones conduct theirs in-house. Most have lavish short-course centres. Junior management receives more training than middle management, with programmes that are product or function specific such as safety at work or quality assurance. For mid-management, courses are company specific and senior management undertake courses which relate mainly to the company and its environment. Medium size companies use the Chambers of Industry and Commerce for their courses. These are wide ranging, and use staff hired from the large companies, polytechnics and universities.

Immigrant workers

Germany has made agreements with many countries on the recruitment and placement of foreign workers – Gastarbeiter – who came from relative poverty to perform mundane, dangerous or dirty tasks that the Germans did not relish themselves. They came from mainly Turkey, and then Yugoslavia, Italy, Greece, Spain and Portugal. They are generally unpopular with Germans who had expected young, single, hard-working men who would pay taxes, and leave within a few years, whereas in reality many have stayed, and brought wives and children, who cost the state for education, etc.

Trade unions

Sixteen unions, one for each large industry, were formed after the war and the Gewerkschaft der Polizei (Police Trade Union) made 17. All are affiliated to the Deutscher Gewerkschaftsbund (DGB), the Confederation of German Trade Unions, which was founded in 1949 to co-ordinate the activities of its members, advise on legal and social security matters, contribute to education and training matters and act as spokesman in national matters. It is not affiliated to any political party, nor associated with any church. It is run by a Federal Board – 28 members: a President, two Vice-Presidents, and 17 Presidents of the member unions, eight full-time officials (heads of special committees). The Federal Congress meets every three years and is attended by 504 delegates.

Firms are legally obliged to have worker representatives on their supervisory boards and there are also works' councils, which are taken very seriously. Collective bargaining takes place between the trade union and the corresponding employers' associations. Once signed, the agreements are legally binding. Trade unions are so integrated into corporate structures that the employers and unions refer to themselves as Sozialpartner, which does indicate a close relationship.

Few days are normally lost through disputes. This is because from reconstruction, employers and unions worked together to achieve higher output. However, there are signs that attitudes are changing, and people want to take life easier – spending more time with their families and taking more holidays, but they do not want to trade more leisure time for less wages. The introduction of more machinery and industrial robots in manufacturing plants has also alienated many workers, so potential conflict exists. This is illustrated by IG Metall (Metal Workers' Union), which in 1984 held an eight week strike over the length of the working week, and this issue is likely to continue to cause friction. There is also debate over the need for weekend work.

The old East German trade union movement has not always integrated well into this system, and is trying hard to gain wage parity with the west. This has almost been achieved, and could cause problems to the new nation.

Greece

Education and training

Children start school at the age of five, and spend a minimum of six years at primary school and three years at secondary school. At the moment, there are discussions about increasing the compulsory secondary education to four years. It is possible to stay on at school for another three years to gain a qualification for further education. Students may attend a university which offers degree courses in the traditional academic subjects usually lasting four years. Polytechnic courses are more vocationally orientated, and normally last for three years, plus six months in the workplace, and result in a national diploma validated by the state. In 1994, about 170,000 students sat the examinations for admittance to higher education, and 42,500 were accepted. Of these, just over half went to university and the remainder to polytechnic.

It is possible for adults to study part-time, often at night schools, but these tend to be lower level courses. Universities and polytechnics do not offer part-time courses. There are private colleges which recruit students who wish to stay in Greece but have not gained a place at university. They award qualifications from overseas institutions. Some firms, especially the multi-nationals, offer training in-house, but the concept of regular training for employees has not yet gained much ground in Greece.

Trade unions

Trade unions are organised on an industry-wide basis, and are co-ordinated through the Greek General Confederation of Labour, which has government recognition. It makes general agreements with the government and employers' associations, and then the unions negotiate with individual firms for even better terms. The level of industrial disputes varies with right-wing governments having to face more strikes than left-wing governments. There is extensive legislation concerning workers, including a minimum wage and employment protection. Consultation between employees and management is normal.

Ireland

Education and Training

Education is compulsory from the ages of six to 15, though many stay on at school after that. The Irish education system concentrates on providing a sound base of numeracy and literacy. There has been little emphasis on training until recently. University education was in the traditional subjects, and many vocational courses were ignored. The result was that many students went elsewhere, especially the UK, to undertake courses in business, agriculture, etc. The response has been the creation of regional technical colleges, which are similar to the old polytechnics in England. These follow on from the original Limerick Regional Technical College which linked its courses to the nearby Business Park so as to ensure relevance and the co-operation of industry. This was a ground-breaking development in Ireland. A similar institution in Dublin followed, tying the courses to the needs of Dublin. Although places remain limited, Ireland is responding to the need for a trained and educated workforce.

Trade unions

Traditionally, the Irish trade union movement has been powerful, and its excessive wage demands have, in the past, prevented some foreign investment, but this attitude has improved in recent years. Nevertheless, the confrontational approach remains common. Extensive legislation exists over working conditions and employment protection.

Italy

Education and training

Education is compulsory for eight years with elementary school (scuola elementare) from six to 11, the secondary school (scuola media inferiore) from 11 to 14, which is the minimum school leaving age. After that, secondary education (scuola media superiore) is diversified with academic, technical or vocational routes. The secondary education system is not regarded as a good preparation for the world of work.

About 10% of the population are at university, with almost one-third taking economics and social studies, one-fifth studying literature, almost one-fifth taking law, and the rest engineering and science. However, over two-thirds of the first year intake of about 250,000 drop out. This could be because there is no selection process.

Apprenticeships remain in the craft industries but have disappeared in other occupations as the trade unions objected to them as exploitation of the young. There is no publicly financed vocational training, except where it is directly linked to the workplace and little adult training available. A few large firms, such as Fiat and Olivetti, have their own training services for new workers, internal transfers and those being considered for promotion. There are few business schools. The private Luigi Bocconi University in Milan has one – the Scuola di Direzione Aziendale. There are wide regional differences in employment, and high unemployment rates for the young and women.

Trade unions

Most employers belong to an employers' association, which include: Confindustria (liberal, free market beliefs); Confcommercio (merchants); Confapi (small firms); Confagricoltura (agricultural producers); Confartigianato (craft industries) and Intersind (for public sector employers).

The unions include: Confederazione Generale Italiana del Lavoro (CGIL), mainly communist; Confederazione Italiana Sindicati Lavoratori (CISL), catholic; Unione Italiana del Lavoro (UIL), smaller than the other two, a mixture of socialist and other parties. The Statute on Workers' Rights (Statuto dei Diritti dei Lavoratori) of 1970 allowed security of employment in large firms.

In the 1970s the Confederation of the three trade unions achieved many successes, including a wage indexation system, wage increases, the 40 hour week and the reduction of wage differentials which led them to demand a role in the management of the economy as a whole, together with claims for higher wages which the employers and the government opposed. In 1980 Fiat dismissed 14,000 workers in a rationalisation so the metal workers section of the union Confederation called an unsuccessful strike. More bitter disputes preceded the break up of the Confederation of the three trade unions, after which the trade union movement went into a decline, and membership fell in the early and mid 1980s.

Pay and conditions are negotiated nationally between the trade unions and the relevant employer's federation with contracts for each industry, and additional plant-level agreements if necessary. They last for three years and stipulate holidays (usually four weeks and ten public holidays), wages, working hours, and permissible levels of overtime. The national agreements are binding only on those employers who sign them, but most do.

Labour law and social security legislation is extensive and detailed. Legislation deals with employment conditions and rights, working conditions, wages, pay and holidays, etc. It ensures that discrimination on racial, sexual or religious grounds is illegal, or on trade union membership or activity and establishes grounds for dismissal. It even identifies four classes of employee: dirigenti (senior managers), quadri (middle managers), impiegati (white collar workers) and operai (manual workers).

Luxembourg

Education and training

Education is provided by the state from the age of six to 15. There are also fee paying schools, most notably the European school and the American school. Education is compulsory up to the age of fifteen, but most people stay at school after this undertaking academic or vocational courses. The vocational courses involve time spent in the workplace. There is a University centre whose one year courses are recognised by foreign universities as the equivalent to the first term of university. Students then usually go to universities in Belgium, France or Germany to obtain a degree. The local workforce is skilled, and is boosted by commuters from France and Belgium who often undertake the less-skilled jobs.

Trade unions

There are three main trade unions: the Chambre du Travail (Council of Labour), the Chambre des Employés Privés (Council of Staff Employees) and the Chambre des Fonctionnaires Publics (Council of National and Local Government Officials). They are actively involved in discussions over regulations and legislation dealing with their members. Detailed legislation exists to deal with the rights of employees. This includes conditions of work, hours and social welfare benefits. In addition, there are comprehensive conciliation arrangements at factory and national level, and every firm with more than 12 workers has a workers' delegation to investigate complaints and act as mediator. Employees are represented on the Board of Directors. The result is that there are no labour problems in Luxembourg.

Netherlands

The proportion of employed women is relatively low; they are paid less than men, and often are employed in low-status jobs.

Education

Schools are funded publicily but are independent of state control. Education is compulsory at primary and secondary levels, after which students may leave, but most stay on, either to pursue academic studies leading to university entrance or more vocational courses. There are seven universities with two more in formation, and three technical universities. They admit all students who have passed the grammar school final examination, which means large lectures, high drop-out rates and long courses. There are vocational courses at the technical universities, both full and part time. Most managers are graduates, usually with such qualifications.

Trade unions

The unions are organised according to branches of industry and commerce, not by craft, so there are few unions and fewer demarcation disputes. Compromise is endemic so labour disputes are rare. Amalgamations in 1976 created the Federatie Nederlandsche Vakbeweging (Federation of Dutch Trade Unions) with almost 900,000 members. The Christelijk Nationaal Vakverbond (CNV) is another federation of trade unions. It has a Catholic orientation. After the war, wage negotiations involved the government as well as employers and labour, but the role of government has effectively disappeared. A minimum wage exists for employees aged 23–65 and there are generous benefits. All firms with 35 or more employees are legally obliged to have a works' council to advise on decisions and for firms with over 100, the council has to be consulted on all important issues, with a right of veto on personnel matters. The closed shop is unknown, and only about 30% of workers are members of unions.

Norway

Education and training

Primary education is compulsory between the ages of seven and 13, and secondary education extends from 13 to 16. The age for beginning school will fall to six in the near future. The aim is to impart knowledge and promote personal development by encouraging practical skills. Over 95% of all 16 year olds stay on at school, to either continue their academic education or undertake vocational training. Most apprentices follow a vocational training course for one or two years and continue for one or two years in the workplace. The National Council for vocational training advises the Ministry of Education, Research and Church Affairs. Each trade or group of trades has a training council, and each county a vocational training committee that administers the apprenticeship system and the examinations, and also offers advice and information on vocational training.

Norway has four universities and six colleges specialising respectively in agriculture, business, veterinary medicine, sport, music and architecture. In addition, there are regional colleges so as to make higher education accessible to all. Adult education has a high priority, and this includes occupational qualifications. These are particularly well-attended at the moment, because of the unemployment in Norway. In 1992, 66,000 people participated in such courses. Thus, the Norwegian system tries to ensure a sound basic education, with vocational training available for all ages.

Trade unions

The largest central unions are the Norwegian Federation of Trade Unions (LO), the Confederation of Vocational Unions (YS) and the Federation of Professional Associations (AF). Employers have their own organizations, the largest of which is the Confederation of Norwegian Business and Industry (NHO). Every year, the unions negotiate with the appropriate employers' organization over conditions and wages. Once agreed, neither side can seek to change it, so strikes are only possible before the agreement is made.

The Working Environment Act lays down workers' rights on working conditions, pay, holidays, etc.

Portugal

Education and training

Basic education is compulsory and consists of three cycles, lasting for four, two, and three years respectively. Secondary education is not compulsory and lasts for three years, and can be either academic or vocational. In the final year, students can take the PGA which is used for university entrance. The higher education system is organised into universities, which offer mainly the more traditional academic subjects, and the polytechnics, which are more vocational. The systems are linked, so that it is possible to transfer from one to another. There are also private higher education institutions.

Trade unions

There is a legal minimum wage and extensive labour legislation dealing with conditions, rights, etc. It is difficult to dismiss a worker. There are two trade union confederations, the left wing CGTP and the more moderate UGT. Unions do not have strike funds, and social security is not available for strikers, so stoppages, although common, seldom last more than two days. Public employees' pay is held down, and the government issues guidelines for the private sector. The Ministry of Labour sets minimum wages for each sector.

Spain

There was emigration of labour from Spain during Franco's reign, together with migration from country to town and from the poorer areas to the wealthier. There has been a fall in the birth rate, and fewer marriages since the legalisation of divorce and abortion in 1985, though there are few divorces and little illegitimacy. The falling birth rate reduced the work force. Madrid and other cities have suffered from a fall in the numbers of young people, which threatens business recruitment. There has been a significant decline in the agricultural workforce (1960, 39%; 1991, 14%), a static manufacturing sector (23%) and rising service sector (31%–54%).

Education and training

Six to 14 year olds study the compulsory Basic General Education (EGB), then there is a two year academic course or vocational training. This causes problems, as parents will insist on repeating years so as to reach the more academic routes, and the vocational certificate has not been readily accepted by employers.

A one year pre-university course (COU), involves Spanish language and literature, a foreign language, mathematics and three optional subjects. There are almost one million university students, in accommodation designed for many less than that number. There are 34 universities, with staff shortages in business and management and technology. There is also the National University for Distance Learning, but it lacks funds and only has about 60,000 registered students. The government plans to modernise the university system to ensure better standards, and encourage the development of courses appropriate to the needs of industry. Business Schools are emerging, but there are insufficient places.

Research expenditure is low, and again the government plans to tackle this by establishing a research base in industry linked to the universities and government research councils. The National Institute for Unemployment (INEM) has recently increased its expenditure on training, especially in new technology and collaborative ventures with trade unions.

Trade unions

There has emerged a free trade union system which includes the communist Comisiones Obreras (Workers' Commissions) and the socialist General Union of Workers (UGT). The unions blame the government for job losses, and reject the government promotion of low wages as an attraction to foreign investment. The two unions compete for members. Figures are not reliable, but only about 20% of the work force appear to have joined the unions which are not well-organised.

Sweden

86% of men and 83% of women work, as two incomes are needed to maintain a decent standard of living. In 1993, official unemployment was 7.5%, with a further 5% being trained but these figures are rising.

Education and training

Primary education is compulsory between the ages of seven to 13, and secondary education extends from 13 to 16. Most sixteen year olds stay on at school, to either continue their academic education or undertake vocational training. Most apprentices follow a vocational training course for one or two years and continue for one or two years in the workplace.

Sweden has universities and colleges specialising in vocational subjects. In addition, there are regional colleges which make higher education accessible to all. Adult education has a high priority, and this includes occupational qualifications. Schemes are available for active job seekers over 20 to acquire requisite skills. The trainee receives a payment plus a subsidy to cover the costs of attending the training. There are also about 250 labour market courses of diverse types.

Trade unions

Collective bargaining agreements determine wages and regulate working conditions. There are a variety of industrial relation laws. The Co-Determination Act gives workers the right to determine jointly with their employers questions concerning the management of their work place. Advance warning must be given of major changes in the organization which could affect employment. The Security of Employment Act (LAS) makes it very difficult to end employment. Social benefits are extensive, and include payments for unemployment and disability benefits, paid maternity leave and child allowances.

The Work Environment Act 1977 was intended to make the work place healthier. The Working Hours Act 1982 limits hours to 40 with no more than 50 hours of overtime per month or 200 per year. The Annual Leave Act gives a minimum of 25 days paid leave per year, plus statutory public holidays.

The Swedish Employers' Confederation in the private sector has 45,000 members, employing 1.4 million people. There are also associations for co-operative employers, publicly owned companies, banks and publishers of periodicals. The Confederation of Professional Employees for white collar workers has 1.3 million members, and the Trade Union Confederation represents 2.3 million or 90% of blue collar workers. There is also the Confederation of Professional Associations with 350,000 members. Labour relations are traditionally good. The unions and employers' associations negotiate national agreements, and recommend them to local employers and unions. These are usually accepted, even by non-members. Signatories renounce strikes and lock outs. Even without an agreement, formal warning must be given of any industrial action.

Switzerland

About 50% of the population work. Foreign nationals account for about 25% of the workforce. They mainly come from Italy, Spain, France and Germany. However, work permits for foreigners are hard to obtain which adds to a skills shortage, and pushes up wages.

Education and training

Education is the responsibility of the cantons, so that there is no single Swiss system. The decentralisation was intended to allow the development of systems that reflect local needs. Nevertheless, there are some common features. Kindergarten is voluntary, but available for all children. Most cantons require nine years compulsory education. Almost all of the youngsters continue their education either in vocational or academic training. The vocational training involves practical work experience and education. It lasts between two and four years and is completed by a certificate of proficiency. The details of the training and examinations for each profession are stipulated by federal government authorities. The more academic route prepares students for university entrance or for professional study.

Universities exist to allow the more traditional type of study, but those wishing to extend their vocational knowledge and skills may attend polytechnics and higher vocational schools. Alternatively, there are advanced trade examinations and higher professional qualifications. All can be taken full or part time. Many firms insist on training, and the promotion system depends upon appropriate qualifications, so that the Swiss workforce is highly trained and capable.

Trade unions

There are no closed shops. In 1937, unions renounced militant action and employers and employees agreed to resolve conflict by discussion. The recession has strained this arrangement, but it has been maintained, and there has been no significant organised strike since 1937. Between 1970 and 1985, 1.7 working days per year per 1,000 employees were lost through strikes, compared to 51 in Germany and 1,276 in Italy. If a strike occurs, the District Labour Court will conciliate. Federal and Canton officials cannot strike, by law.

The three largest unions are the Swiss Federation of Labour Unions with about 440,000 members, the Christian National Federation of Labour

Unions with about 115,000 and the white collar Association of Employees Federations with around 145,000. Only about 35% of workers are members, but unions are important, and negotiate wages with the appropriate employers' association, and the result is binding. In addition, the federal government consults the unions and employers associations before introducing legislation.

United Kingdom

Education and training

Education is compulsory from the age of five to 16, after which students can stay on to receive an academic education, undertake vocational courses, or enter the labour market. Criticisms of low levels of numeracy and literacy, poor general knowledge and lack of preparation for work in the school system led to the 1988 Education Reform Act which introduced a national curriculum intended to ensure that all children gained a thorough knowledge of English, maths and science. Some control was taken away from local authorities who fund the schools, and given to governors and the head.

At the same time, the National Council of Vocational Training was introduced to provide qualifications based on occupational competence. This has meant that an increasing number of the many students entering higher education have vocational rather than academic entry qualifications. It is hoped that this will improve the technical and supervisory workforce in the future.

The Youth Training Scheme was introduced in 1983. In 1988, there were 435,000 youngsters involved but many had problems with numeracy and literacy and jobs were not always available on completion. From April 1988, every organization applying to participate has had to have Approved Training Organization status. In May 1990, YTS was replaced by Youth Training, administered at local level by Training Enterprise Councils. For adults, the Job Training Scheme was replaced in 1988 by Employment Training, which rapidly attracted 200,000 participants. It offers up to a year's training, as well as training in the work place. By 1991, there were 82 TECs in England and Wales and 22 LECs (Local Enterprise Companies, the Scottish equivalent) in Scotland. The Management Charter Initiative was established to encourage management training. By 1991, over 800 leading companies had pledged their support, but the initial impetus has receded.

Trade unions

In the 1970s many employers were frightened of trade unions; this attitude had disappeared by the early 1990s. In the late 1970s and early 1980s, the amount of time lost through strikes grew so Mrs Thatcher's Conservative Government passed several Acts of Parliament which were intended to limit the power of the unions, and so reduce the number of strikes.

The number of trade unions has declined greatly in recent years, so that now there are now fewer than 300 trade unions in the UK, many of which do not have large memberships. The biggest unions have been formed as a result of amalgamations between smaller unions, such as the Transport and General Workers Union which has nearly 1.25 million members. Most unions are affiliated to the Trades Union Congress (TUC), which is the central body of the trade union movement. It holds an annual conference which decides on general policy, although the individual unions can ignore the decisions if they wish. The TUC has recognised that the increased socialist presence of the European Parliament could lead to improved, standardised European conditions for its members. The membership of trade unions has declined greatly in recent years, but nevertheless about 40% of workers in the UK are members of trade unions. Some industries have more than this, and some less. For example, most coal miners are members of a union, but the hotel and catering industry does not have high membership. It is higher among full-time than part-time workers, among men than women, and in large rather than small firms.

Activity

- ☐ The students continue to investigate their chosen European country.
- ☐ Using the approach adopted in the chapter, the students should once more then decide on the information that would be required in order to include this country in the chapter.
- ☐ They should then again decide what sources they should consult in order to compile the information.
- ☐ The information is likely to be extremely difficult to obtain, and so the students will require guidance at the preparation stage. Indeed, it may well be that they will need to be provided with some sources.
- ☐ Armed with these, the students should be given time to gather and analyse the required information and make a presentation to their contemporaries.
- ☐ They should indicate their sources and, especially if there are gaps in their work, explaiin the difficulties that they encountered.
- ☐ The sources are likely to be varied, and there is considerable scope for students to demonstrate initiative and skill in the collection of relevant data.
- ☐ Thus, this exercise represents a further development from those already set.

Chapter Seven

Marketing in the European Union

Aims of this chapter

□ To look at the differences in the selling and buying procedures in each country in the European Union
□ To identify the main media that can be used for advertising including newspapers and periodicals, radio and television, cinemas and posters
□ To consider the attitudes prevalent within each country including the ability to speak different languages, social customs, and differences which may exist between young and old, city dwellers and rural inhabitants
□ To establish the best ways to behave if wishing to export to each country, including polite behaviour, suitable dress, methods of greetings, etc.

To sell goods from one member state to another within the European Union ought to be a simple and straightforward affair. Legislation has been passed to ensure that all of the companies within the Union can compete with each other without hindrance. The EEC Treaty emphasises the importance of fair competition, and Article 85(1) forbids companies from limiting, preventing or distorting competition within the Union. This is aimed particularly at price fixing and agreements on market share. Article 30 forbids the use of quotas on products from other member states. The European Court of Justices has debarred import licences, and even the discrimination between domestic and foreign goods.

In the past, many central and local governments have bought goods from within their own country. Directives sought to end this by insisting on open tendering, which allowed any supplier to bid for a government contract, or restricted tendering, which allowed only approved suppliers to bid, but which allowed any supplier to apply for approved status. These directives were not successful, so that further measures were introduced, including the Compliance Directive of 1991, which allowed for action to be taken against breaches.

Different technical standards have been used to prevent trade, but the Single European Act harmonised technical standards so that goods accepted in one country had to be accepted in all, so it ceased to be acceptable to use technical standards as a barrier.

However, the competition policy is not necessarily successful, in that its implementation is partly in the hands of the Commission and partly individual governments, and so there is no clear, single line on the problem. Moreover, the Commission can only act on receiving a complaint, and cannot otherwise investigate what it regards as potential breaches. Even if it had such powers, it lacks the staff and the financial resources to tackle the matter adequately. No doubt changes will take place in the future to ensure that the union's policy of fair competition is obeyed. However, anyone seeking to sell in a new market place needs to know something about the attitudes of the people. This chapter attempts to look at the media of each country, and the peculiarities of the people.

Austria

The Austrian economy is strong, and the people enjoy a high standard of living, which means that the consumer market is relatively large, and also competitive. Austria's German-speaking neighbours, Germany and Switzerland, share its desire for reliable, durable products, and are traditional trading partners. Austrian consumers expect a high level of personal service, so the market is dominated by smaller, specialised retail outlets, though supermarkets and chain stores are increasingly popular.

The media

There is no national press. Each province tends to have a socialist, a conservative and an independent paper. Vienna has more papers, including the *Wiener Zeitung* (Government Gazette) and *Der Kurier* and *Die Neue Kronen Zeitung* which reach the provinces. Circulations are low. The weekend editions are larger, and carry extensive advertising. There are weekly magazines and many trade and technical papers. Broadcasting is administered through a corporation established by the state and owned by the Federal and Provincial Governments. There are some sponsored programmes and set advertising slots. Cinemas allow advertising. There are good poster sites in the towns. These are usually controlled by the municipalities.

The ethos

Visits by senior executives are invaluable, and the ability to speak German is much appreciated. Business is conducted on a formal basis. Punctuality is expected, and business cards are exchanged. The use of formal titles is of particular importance. It is usual to exchange social pleasantries for a few minutes before discussing business. Austrians are usually formal in their social lives. First names are not used when people first meet. Handshaking on meeting and departure is normal. The Church is much respected in Austria, and all visitors should remember this.

Belgium

Belgium is one of the most prosperous countries in Europe, with a very high standard of living. The market is competitive, and the consumer expects quality goods and services. Tastes do not vary much between the communities and are often regarded as rather conservative. Family life is very important and Belgians take great pride in their homes, and so spend large amounts of money on household goods. This includes appliances such as washing machines and fridges, but also tables and cutlery, and even board games. Spending on clothes, on the other hand, is relatively low. The growth of supermarkets and hypermarkets has reduced significantly the number of specialist shops, though many small fresh food outlets have survived. Belgians are large consumers of meat, with pork being especially popular but lamb a rarity.

The media

There are a large number of low circulation daily papers in French and Flemish. The most widely read are *Le Soir* and *La Libre Belgique* (in French) and *De Standaar/Het Nieuwsblad* and *Het Laatste Nieuws* (in Flemish). There are a wide variety of trade journals. Commercial advertising is allowed on Belgian state radio and television. There are also 40 cable companies operating 150 local or regional radio and television networks. Cinemas are a normal medium for advertising. Posters are used for advertising in railway stations and on the roadside, and even the sides of buses and trams may carry adverts.

The ethos

There are many small firms, which means that anyone going to Belgium to try to sell goods may meet a senior member of the firm, who can take immediate decisions, so the representative must have similar authority. Suits should be worn for business meetings, which will be formal.

Punctuality is expected, and business cards are exchanged. The Flemish may prefer to speak to visitors from the UK in English rather than French.

Denmark

The Danish market is sophisticated, and although tastes are similar to those in the UK, greater emphasis is placed on design and quality. Large amounts of money are spent on home furnishings and electrical appliances.

The media

There are 46 main dailies with a combined circulation of almost 1.7 million. The most important are the *Berlingske Tidende*, *Politiken* and *Aktuelt*. Women's magazines are popular. There are also about 600 trade journals. There are two main television channels. The state owned Danmarks Radio has no advertising. The commercial channel is TV2, which has between seven and 13 advertising slots a day, not exceeding 10% of transmission time. There is also local television which can broadcast for a limited number of hours per day. The cinema is popular in Denmark. Advertising uses humour. The advertisements may be the same as on television, but cinema often promotes more international products. Illuminated neon signs and paintings on the sides of buildings are commonly used for advertising but posters are not common. Advertisements appear on the railways, in buses, taxis and telephone kiosks.

The ethos

Most Danes speak English well. German is the next most-favoured language. The Danes are proud of their country and do not like to be confused with other Scandinavian countries. They are delighted if visitors demonstrate some knowledge and appreciation of their country. The German occupation of Denmark during the Second World War should not be mentioned in conversation. Personal visits by customers are regarded as particularly important in Denmark. Punctuality is extremely important, and the approach to business is direct. Guests should refrain from drinking until the host toasts the health of the guest.

Finland

The Finns enjoy a high standard of living, and expect goods to be of good quality. The market is keenly price-competitive and purchasers expect goods to be delivered promptly.

The media

There are over 100 daily papers with 3.1 million readers. The most significant are *Helsingin Sanomeat* (480,000), *Ilta Sanomat* (evening paper, 215,000) and *Aamulehta* (145,000). There are financial and trade papers including *Kauppalehti* (five times a week, 84,000), *Tekniikka* and *Talous* (three times a week, 95,000), *Talouselama* (54,000). There are three national television channels and one regional channel operated by Oy Yleisradio Ab, the government-controlled national broadcasting company. Time is rented to a commercial television advertising company, MTV Oy. There is also state-run radio, and a large number of commercial, regional stations. There are 350 cinemas in the country and 46 in Helsinki alone, which makes them an ideal vehicle for advertising. Poster advertising is handled by specialist firms.

The ethos

Only 6% of the population speak Swedish, but many of these have responsible positions in industry and commerce. English is widely spoken in the country as a whole and within the business community in particular. Businessmen are expected to dress smartly. Punctuality is essential for both business and social appointments. Visiting cards are considered polite. Handshaking is normal. Finns may appear reserved, so there may be an absence of small talk on first meeting. Guests should refrain from drinking until the host toasts the health of the guest.

France

Although the French have a reputation for buying domestically produced goods, France is one of the world's largest importers of consumer goods. The French market is competitive and sophisticated. Goods are of high quality in terms of performance and appearance. Design and style are often more important than price. The amount spent on household appliances is relatively large. Hypermarkets have developed very rapidly in France, and many specialist outlets have disappeared. French cuisine is world famous, but expenditure on tinned meat and fish is very high. Paris is the largest single market, but well over half of the population live outside the main conurbations, so exporters need to make special efforts to develop sales in the regions.

The media

There are a large number of newspapers, though few have a national circulation. Daily papers include *Le Figaro* (circulation about 425,000), *Le Monde* (circulation 385,000, with about 40,000 sold abroad), *Le Parisien*

(385,000), *France Soir* (250,000) and *L'Equipe* (a daily sports paper, circulation 300,000). The weekly papers enjoy a wider, more national, circulation, and include *L'Express* (580,000), *Paris Match* (875,000), *Le Nouvel Observateur* (360,000) and *Le Canard Enchaîné* (a satirical magazine, circulation 420,000). All of these papers are based in the area round Paris. There are many regional papers, including *Ouest-France*, based in Rennes (800,000), *La Voix du Nord*, based in Lille (370,000), *Sud Ouest*, based in Bordeaux (370,000). French television was for many years a government monopoly, but is now a mixture of public and commercial channels. Advertising is allowed on all channels, but the public channels receive much of their revenue from a licence fee. French radio allows advertising on its public channels, and there are also commercial radio stations. Advertising takes place in cinemas and posters are common.

The ethos

Businessmen dress conservatively. Meetings are by appointment, and business cards are exchanged. The French prefer to converse in their own language, and it is considered rude to commence a conversation in French and then switch to another language. Business meetings tend to be formal, and decisions taken only after lengthy discussion. Business entertainment in restaurants is common. Handshakes are normal on meeting and departure. The use of the terms Monsieur and Madame is common, and it may take some time before Christian names are introduced. Meal times can be long and leisurely and guests are expected to show appreciation of French food and wine.

Germany

The new taxes levied to pay for unification have reduced disposable incomes and thus slowed private consumption in the West. Nevertheless, the West remains an affluent and demanding market. Merchandise must be of thhe highest quality and styled to meet consumer taste. The Germans are status conscious and will pay premium prices for quality accompanied by sound maintenance, service, guarantee and delivery. Many of the regions are distinctive. For example, the pattern of consumption between Munich and Hamburg is very different, so regional tastes must be considered. Large retail groups have replaced many small independent operators.

The media

There are about 10,000 newspapers and periodicals in Germany. About 4,000 are trade, technical or scientific, usually published monthly, but with long lead times for publication. There are a large number of regional newspapers with relatively low circulations – 375 dailies in the West alone. Relatively few newspapers have a national circulation. The 12 page tabloid *BILD* sells over five million, but advertising space is limited. The other major national dailies have circulations of 200,000–540,000, including *Die Welt* (Bonn, 217,000), *Frankfurter Allgemeine Zeitung* (Frankfurt, 398,000), *Süddeutsche Zeitung* (Munich 397,000). In the East, the major papers are *Sächsische Zeitung* (Dresden 457,000), *Thüringer Allgemeine* (Erfurt 537,000), *Freie Presse* (Chemnitz 519,000). *Der Spiegel* is a weekly news magazine; *Die Zeit* is a weekly with an intellectual readership. Weekly glossies with circulations in excess of one million are *Stern* (Hamburg) and *Bunte Illustrierte* (Munich). The main German television network, Arbeitsgemeinschaft der Öffentlichen Rundfunkanstalten Deutschlands (ARD) is a group effort from 11 public broadcasting companies and there is another state-sponsored channel, Zweites Deutsches Fernsehen (ZDF). Both ARD and ZDF allow advertising but it is restricted to 6pm–8pm, excluding Sundays. There are about 2,000 cinemas, and special publicity films are often shown. Advertising is to be found on billboards on public transport, and even displays in public toilets.

The ethos

German businessmen dress smartly. Appointments should be made in advance, and punctuality is vital. Handshaking is normal. Formal titles are used. Common courtesies are important. For example, you should issue a greeting on entering a shop and say goodbye on leaving. To do otherwise is considered rude. When making a telephone call, it is important to say who you are before asking to speak to someone. Germans tend to speak good English but are pleased if you make an effort to use their language. They also like to meet the senior executives of the companies with whom they deal.

Greece

Greece is one of the less prosperous countries in Western Europe, and has experienced many changes in the post-war period, including large scale migration from the countryside to the towns, temporary migration to other countries, and the rapid growth of tourism. This has led to new spending patterns, with the retail sector coming closer to the rest of Europe. However, purchases of household equipment, apart from cookers, fridges and freezers, are relatively low. Spending on cars and clothes is also low. Supermarkets and multiple stores are growing in number and selling heavily advertised branded goods but a very large number of small family businesses remain, selling low volumes of goods. Distribution costs are high, as are the mark-ups on goods. It is the ambition of most Greeks to be sellf-employed, which will reduce the speed of change to larger establishments.

The media

There are 14 national dailies published in Athens, and two in Salonica. The most popular are: in the morning, *Acropolis*, *Kathimerini*, and *Makedonia* (Salonica), and in the afternoon, *Ethnos*, *Ta Nea*, *Apogevmatini*, *Eleftherotypia*, *Vrathini*, *Avriani*, *Eleftheros Typos*, *Messimvrini* and *Thessalonika* (Salonica). No newspaper has a circulation over 150,000. There are financial daily papers – *Naftemboriki* and *Express*, and the weekly *Economicos Tachidromos* – and trade magazines. There are two government-sponsored broadcasting corporations, Hellenic Radio and Television (ERT1 and ERT2), which operate nationally and allow advertising. There are commercial and regional television channels, and a large network of commercial radio stations. Cinemas are widely used for advertising and posters are a normal method of advertising.

The ethos

Formal suits are expected when conducting business. Handshaking is a normal courtesy. Business meetings may be lengthy, with a variety of subjects discussed. English, French and German are widely spoken. Greeks are very proud of their country, and there is a strong sense of unity. The Greek Orthodox Church has a strong influence, especially in rural areas, and visitors should be careful not to offend the religious inclinations of the people. Greece is an old-fashioned country, and there may be differences in attitude between the young and the old, the city dweller and those from agricultural areas.

Ireland

The Irish market is similar, but not identical, to that of the UK. There has been a rapid growth in supermarket chains, especially in the grocery sector. Purchases of electrical household goods are increasing, but car sales are low.

The media

The national papers include the *Irish Times*, the *Irish Independent*, and the tabloid *The Press*. There are Sunday papers, including *Sunday World*, which specialises in scandals, and has a wide readership. There are many local papers covering the country. Perhaps the most significant is the *Cork Examiner*. British papers are available in towns and cities. Television is broadcast through the two semi-state-owned channels RTE1 and 2, which were only established in the early 1960s. They receive their revenue from a licence fee and advertising. There is a similar arrangement for radio, as well as a large number of private local commercial stations. Broadcasts from the UK can be received in most areas. The cinemas are popular throughout the country and, therefore, are important for advertising. Posters are another traditional form of advertising.

The ethos

Business people wear smart clothes. Meetings are friendly and informal, and can last a long time. The Irish are gregarious and welcoming. Ireland is a close community and links can easily be established with people living many miles apart. Abortion, divorce and homosexuality remain illegal and contraception has only recently been allowed. This gives an idea of the influence of the church on the country, especially in rural areas, so visitors must be careful not to offend the beliefs of the nation. There are wide differences between the attitudes of the town and the country, the east and the west, the young and the old, so that it is impossible to establish a single Irish attitude. However, the enjoyment of life, the friendliness and the genuine warmth of the people to visitors is common to the whole of Ireland. The issue of Northern Ireland should be avoided in conversation and non-committal replies are most appropriate if the issue arises. The history of Anglo-Irish affairs does not always reflect well on the English, and strong feelings can be aroused.

Italy

Italy's market is fragmented, with marked regional differences. The people of the north are less conservative in their tastes and thus more willing to try new products than those from the south. The family is important, and the spending on food has always been high. In recent years, there has been an increase in purchases of household equipment and appliances. Italians are very fashion conscious and spend a relatively large proportion of their income on clothes. Non-traditional food is beginning to appear in the shops as the Italian starts to experiment with foreign dishes. For all goods, quality must be high to satisfy the demands of the customer.

The media

Italy has about 100 daily newspapers, though three – *Corriere della Sera* (Milan), *La Stampa* (Turin) and *La Repubblica* (Rome) have widespread distribution. There are many periodicals, including news, women's magazines and specialist publications. The business weekly *Il Mondo* has a large circulation. There are about 2,000 high quality specialised trade publications. RAI, the state owned broadcasting corporation, transmits three national television and three national radio channels, all of which carry advertisements. There are many private channels, some national, others more local. There are over 4,000 cinemas in Italy, where filmgoing is popular, so they are important for advertisers. Posters are permitted in built-up areas and along main roads.

The ethos

There are very many small and medium firms, where Italian is likely to be the only language spoken, so a knowledge of Italian is a real advantage everywhere. Prior appointments are needed. Letters should be grammatically correct and styles of greetings are important. There is an emphasis on personal contact rather than letter writing, and this can make the sales process a slow one. There can also be problems resulting from a cumbersome legal system, and a bureaucratic zeal. The social structure is heavily influenced by the Catholic Church, especially in rural areas, and family ties are very strong. However, Italy is a changing country, and the attitudes of the old and the young may be different; the city dwellers may have different beliefs to those living in the countryside.

Luxembourg

Luxembourg has one of the highest standards of living in Europe and the people expect a choice of high-quality products. Spending on clothes and home furnishings and appliances is high. Food consumption, and especially pork produce, is well above average for the EU. Great pride is taken in cars, which are seen as highly prestigious.

The media

The newspapers are published in German, although some articles are in French, and the French daily *Le Républicain Lorrain*, prints a supplement for Luxembourg. The *Luxemburger Wort* has the widest circulation. There are few trade journals produced in the country, but those from elsewhere are widely used. Radio Télé-Luxembourg (RTL) has commercial television networks in French and German, and broadcasts radio programmes. The cinema is used for advertising.

The ethos

Suits are expected for business meetings. Prior appointments should be made, and business cards exchanged. Handshaking is the normal greeting. Business is conducted in a formal manner. Luxembourgers are proud of their country and their national identity, so avoid drawing too many similarities with their neighbours, especially Belgium. An understanding of the history and culture of Luxembourg is much appreciated.

Netherlands

The Netherlands has a very high standard of living, and people expect to buy quality products. Home furnishings and equipment attract a high level of expenditure. There has been a large increase in the number of supermarkets, and a decline in specialist outlets but there is an emphasis on fresh produce rather than tinned and frozen.

The media

The main daily papers are *De Telegraaf* (a conservative morning paper with a circulation of 725,000), *Algemeen Dagblad* (a liberal morning paper with a circulation of 410,000), *Dagblad Trouw* (a protestant, progressive morning paper, circulation 120,000), *NRC/Handelsblad* (a liberal evening paper, circulation 240,000) and *Het Parool* (an independent, socialist evening paper, circulation 100,000). Foreign newspapers are widely available. Since 1928, the responsibility for radio, and later television, programmes has been in the hands of independent organizations. If they have enough members, they can apply for a broadcasting licence. These organizations represent political, religious or educational groups and government agencies. The Netherlands Broadcasting Corporation co-ordinates the programmes, promotes the interest of the organizations, offers technical facilities and makes its own programmes. It allocates broadcasting time, as the organisations do not have their own stations. Since 1992, there has been restricted advertising in the evening. However, the organizations are able to advance their cause during their broadcasts. The main organizations include AVRO, which is non-aligned, NCRV, which is Protestant, VARA, which is Social Democrat, UPRO which is Progressive, and KRO which is Roman Catholic. The cinemas permit advertising, and the use of bill boards is common.

The ethos

Appointments are necessary and visiting cards are exchanged. The handshake is the normal custom. There is an expectation that the members of the commercial and professional community be smartly dressed. The majority of Dutch business people speak good English. Dutch business people are punctual, straightforward and unpretentious and are cautious of those who behave in an ostentatious manner.

Norway

The standard of living in Norway is very high and the wage differentials between socio-economic groups are relatively small. The family unit is important. Norwegians are proud of their country and, as they gained their independence from Sweden in 1905, they do not like to be considered Swedish. English is commonly spoken. Safety is an important issue with the Norwegian consumer. In clothing, blue, red and brown are the biggest sellers, but brighter colours are becoming popular, as are rich, dark colours and tartans. Norwegians are well educated and sophisticated. They expect high quality, and will pay premium prices. The main regional differences in consumption are in the areas of household expenditure, with urban areas spending more on housing, heat and light, drinks and tobacco and other goods and services.

The media

There is no national press in Norway. Those newspapers with the largest circulations are concentrated around the main cities. The papers include *Dagens Naeringsliv* (circulation 52,000), *Aftenposter* (mornings, circulation c275,000, evenings circulation 200,000), *Stavanger Aftenblad* (71,000), *Arbeiderbladet* (44,000), *Adresseavisen* (Trondheim, 90,000), *Bergens Tidente* (95,000), *Dagbladet* (225,000), *Verdens Gang* (375,000). The latter two are tabloids, publishing the more sensational news, and so are suitable for advertising consumer goods. There is a wide variety of regional papers and an important trade press. The Norwegian State Broadcasting Corporation (NRK) runs two television channels, one paid for by licence fee and the other, a commercial channel, by advertisers. There are also commercially financed companies. NRK run four radio channels, and there are also commercial stations. Advertising in the cinemas is normal, but posters are not as common as in some other countries.

The ethos

Business people are expected to dress smartly. Appointments are necessary. Norwegians tend to be formal and may appear reserved. Punctuality is essential. Calling cards are common. Lunch is the main meal of the day, and may be eaten in the late afternoon. Guests should refrain from drinking until the host toasts the health of the guest.

Portugal

Portugal is one of the least affluent countries in Western Europe. Wages are relatively low, and disposable income limited. This means comparitively less consumption, especially on household appliances and clothing.

The media

There are a large number of papers, with a combined readership of only around one million. The following are the most influential: *Diario de Noticias*, *Expresso*, *Tempo*, *Dairio Popular*, *Correia de Manha* and *O Capital*. A trade press exists. There are two state-owned television channels, ITP1 and ITP2, both of which carry advertisements, and two commercial channels. There is state radio and a large number of local commercial stations. Cinemas are used for advertising. Posters are also used for advertising but are not permitted on main roads.

The ethos

English is spoken by many young people, but less so by the older generation. Nevertheless, the ability to speak Portuguese is much appreciated. The Portuguese like to stress their independence from Spain. Business people expect smart dress. Only senior executives exchange visiting cards. The Portuguese way of life is leisurely, and old fashioned politeness is essential. However, there are differences in attitudes between the young and the old, and between urban and rural dwellers, as some of the old traditions are being questioned.

Spain

Spain's rapid economic development over the last 30 years has been ignored by many people, who continue to regard the country as predominantly agricultural. In fact, there has been a large growth in the manufacturing sector and the development of tourism which has allowed Spain to become relatively prosperous. The Spanish take great pride in their families, and children enjoy a higher social profile than in Britain. Furnishings are important, but expenditure on other household goods and clothes is relatively low. However, the retail trade structure has not moved as rapidly as other parts of the economy, and supermarkets have been recent innovations.

The media

Newspapers have limited circulations. The Madrid based dailies *El País*, *ABC*, *Ya*, *El Independiente* and *Diario 16* are available nationally although their circulation outside the main towns and cities is limited. The Barcelona based *Vanguardia*, *El Periodico*, *Diario de Barcelona*, *Avui* and *Día* reach Catalonia and the north east. *El Correo Español* and *Deia* are published in Bilbao and serve the north. The area around Vigo has the *Faro de Vigo*; La Coruna has *La Voz de Galicia* and Seville *ABC* and *El País*. Madrid publishes the economic and business papers *5 Dias* and *Expansión*. There are some weekly illustrated and news magazines such as *Tiempo*, *Cambio 16*, *Tribuna*, *Epoca*, and some women's magazines, but circulations rarely exceed 200,000. There are state-controlled radio and television channels, which allow advertising, as well as regional channels and commercial stations.

The ethos

Business people are expected to dress smartly, though the younger generation may dress slightly less formally than the older executives. They are also more likely to speak English. However, the Spanish appreciate any attempt to employ their language. Business cards are frequently exchanged. Appointments should be made. Spain has made rapid changes in recent years, and many of the older customs are starting to disappear, but hospitality and courtesy remain important. Handshaking is the normal form of greeting. Meetings can be lengthy and formal.

Sweden

Sweden is an affluent country with a sophisticated market which demands goods of high quality. Delivery is important. There are few regional trends. There has been a rapid decline in shop density, especially in rural areas, and an increase in the number of supermarkets, hypermarkets and department stores.

The media

The main national papers are *Dagens Nyheter* (c400,000), *Sevenska Dagbladet* (c200,000), *Goteborgs Posten* (280,000), *Arbetet* (100,000), *Sydsvenska Dagbladet* (southern region 120,000), *Dagens Industri* (business paper, 82,000, week days only), *Expressen* (evening paper 560,000) and *Aftonbladet* (evening paper 375,000). They also publish on Sundays. The evening papers are more sensational and so are better for consumer goods. There is a wide range of local papers. There is an extensive trade and technical press which is often read in English. Advertising is not allowed on public radio and television. There are two commercial channels, but advertising is not dominant. There are poster sites in most towns, but there are limits on the size of advertising posters.

The ethos

Business people are expected to dress smartly. Punctuality is important for business and social occasions. Business cards are common. English is widely spoken. The Swedes may appear somewhat formal and reserved. Guests should refrain from drinking until the host toasts the health of the guest. There is little social ostentation. The family remains important and traditional holidays are observed. Many old customs are retained. For example, red clothing is still popular around Christmas.

Switzerland

Switzerland is an extremely wealthy country whose inhabitants are sophisticated and discerning. Quality, design and finish are of great importance, together with prompt delivery and efficient after-sales. Tastes vary within the country, according to the linguistic area.

The media

Newspapers tend to be regional. The most influential are *Neue Zürcher Zeitung* and *Journal de Genève* with national and international circulations. The German language tabloid *Blick* is the most popular with a circulation of 360,000. All major cities have local papers. There are several high-circulation illustrated magazines appropriate for advertising consumer goods. The trade press includes specialist papers, weekly or monthly, in all three languages. No advertising is permitted on the national Swiss radio networks. However, there are private local stations, with a transmission area limited to 10k radius which can broadcast 40 minutes of advertising a day. There are three national television networks – DRS (German), TSR (French) and TSI (Italian). Advertising is allowed on all three, in three to four minute blocks, four times daily. There are 400 cinemas. Advertising is common. Posters are confined to selected sites. Road side advertising is not allowed.

The ethos

Business people are expected to dress smartly. The Swiss are likely to speak English, but appreciate any attempt to speak the language of the host, especially in the French-speaking areas. Visiting cards are essential. Politeness is expected. Personal visits are important to Swiss businessmen.

United Kingdom

The UK is a relatively wealthy country with a high standard of living. Price remains an important consideration. There is a high level of ownership of leisure electrical appliances. Specialist shops are disappearing with the continued development of supermarkets and hypermarkets.

The media

The UK is one of the few countries with a national press. Tabloids such as *The Sun* and the *Daily Mirror* sell several million copies a day. The more prestigious papers include the *Times*, the *Financial Times*, the *Daily Telegraph*, the *Guardian* and the *Independent*, and there are papers in between the two, such as the *Daily Mail*, *Today* and the *Daily Express*. There are also many national Sunday papers. There is a strong local press, mainly with evening papers. There are magazines such as the *Economist* and *Investor's Chronicle*. The BBC is a public corporation, and has two national television channels and five radio channels. Revenue comes from a licence fee, and there is no advertising. There are two commercial television channels, and regional commercial radio. The cinema is normally used for advertising, and posters are common.

The ethos

Business people are expected to dress smartly. Appointments should be made, and business cards are usually exchanged. English is the normal language, except in Wales, where Welsh or English may be spoken. Handshaking is a formal greeting.

Activity

☐ The students should continue to investigate their chosen European country.

☐ Using the approach adopted in the chapter, the students should then decide on the information that would be required in order to include this country in the chapter.

☐ They should then decide what sources they should consult in order to compile the information.

☐ The information is likely to be difficult to obtain, and so the students could require guidance at the preparation stage.

☐ The students should gain the required information and present to their contemporaries.

☐ They should indicate their sources, and explain any difficulties that they have encountered. The sources are likely to be much more diverse than those encountered in Chapters 1 and 5, and may well include personal experiences, or those of friends and relatives. This can be extremely valuable, but in this case, there is a need to ensure that the sources are up-to-date.

☐ This could again be the basis for an assessment, as it offers the students an opportunity to develop research skills within clear framework. However, the demands are more sophisticated and more difficult to obtain than those in Chapters 1 and 5, and so offer a logical progression in information finding and processing.

Chapter Eight

The UK and Europe

Aims of this chapter

☐ To identify and explain the British attitude during early
post-war years by identifying those issues which shaped
the order of priorities
☐ To examine the reasons for the reluctance of the UK to
participate in the ECSC and British plans for alternative
structures
☐ To show the changing attitude during the 1960s, leading
ultimately to membership of the European Community
in 1973
☐ To show the British stance since accession with particular reference to the late 1980s and early 1990s

Together with Jean Monnet and Robert Schuman, Winston Churchill is
often seen as one of the originators of the European idea. However, it
should be noted that Churchill was less than keen to actually integrate
British sovereignty into any federal European structure. Rather, Churchill
saw Britain and the Commonwealth, along with the United States (and
perhaps even the Soviet Union), as a guarantor of a new political order in
Europe. He made this clear in his now celebrated Zurich speech in
September 1946. Britain was to be benevolent, if rather distant, as far as
Europe was concerned. Why was this so?

It is, of course, tempting to interpret this attitude solely in terms of British
insularity. While there is some substance in such a view, it is nevertheless an
over-simplification. Part of the answer undoubtedly lies in the state of
postwar Britain and in the priorities of the Attlee Government. While
victorious in World War II, Britain nevertheless emerged exhausted and
virtually bankrupt. It is unsurprising that domestic recovery was seen as the

most pressing issue. The Labour Government which came to power in 1945 was committed to a programme of major reforms, such as the introduction of the National Health Service and the nationalisation of key sectors of industry, for example the railways.

Arguably, the state of the Commonwealth – not least given the problems generated by Indian independence – was an issue which could hardly be ignored. The re-establishment of British authority over territories (such as Malaya) which had been overrun and occupied, proved highly problematic –a difficulty faced not only Britain but by other colonial powers, such as the Netherlands and France.

It also seems likely that many in the UK took justifiable pride in the fact that for a year of the war (between the fall of France and the German invasion of the Soviet Union), the UK and Commonwealth had stood alone against Nazi Germany and survived, when allies, such as France and Poland, had been defeated in a matter of weeks. This being so, why did Britain have any need to become actively involved in any proposed integrative structures on the European continent?

Developments such as the European Coal and Steel Community (ECSC) in some ways ran counter to British policy at the time. The Attlee Government had taken both of the industries into state control as part of its programme. To surrender national control in these circumstances would have been difficult even if the Government had possessed the political will to do so. In any event, the Attlee administration proved just as anti-federalist as many of the Euro-sceptics of the 1980s and 1990s.

Britain saw little need to become politically involved in Europe. In view of the experience of two World Wars, it can be argued that European affairs had proved extremely costly to the UK in both human and material terms. If structures were being put in place which would serve to stabilise European relations, then it would be sufficient for Britain to make encouraging gestures from the sidelines and the need for intervention on the Continent would eventually disappear. In any event, Europe was only one factor in the equation which represent Britain's perception of its place in world affairs. Churchill's idea of three overlapping circles perhaps explains this best.

With its strong links to North America (the "special relationship" with the United States), its leading role in the Commonwealth and its proximity in geographical if not political terms to the European continent, the UK could be seen to occupy a unique position – the point where the three circles overlap. The problem with this assessment was, of course, that it rested on the assumption that all three circles represented constants. Subsequent events proved otherwise.

While British indifference can certainly be explained in terms of the above, there are at least three other factors which merit consideration. Firstly, with its traditional status as a trading nation, Britain remained strongly committed to the doctrine of free trade. After all, this had served the country well enough in the past, given its established strengths in

figure 8.1: *The Overlapping Circles*

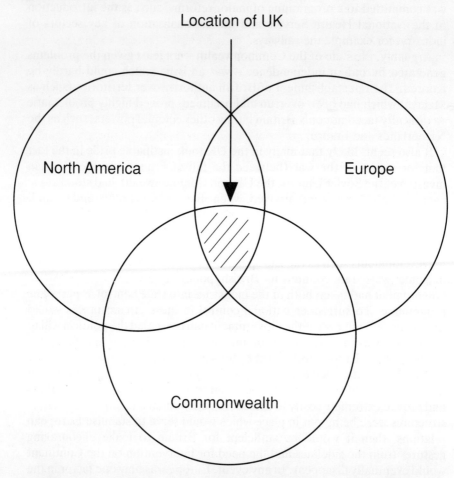

Location of UK

North America

Europe

Commonwealth

manufacturing, banking and merchant shipping. A trading regime un-fettered by regulation had, if anything, served to strengthen Britain's hand. Conversely, the establishment of supra-national authorities would erode British influence.

Secondly, despite the experience of two world wars, which had clearly altered the global balance of military and economic power, Britain was still perceived (both at home and abroad) to be one of the dominant forces in world affairs. If this status now depended to a significant extent on the "special relationship" with Washington, Britain nevertheless remained what might be termed a Great Power with global interests and a global sphere of influence.

Thirdly, we should not underestimate the importance of other psycho-logical factors which influenced the British perception of Europe – even if these are somewhat racist in tone. At this time, many in the UK saw themselves as innately superior to the Europeans, whom they regarded somewhat disdainfully as being unable to manage their own affairs. This inability, it was argued, had led to British involvement in two World Wars in rapid succession and had weakened the country as a result. In any case, few in the UK appeared to believe that proposals for closer economic ties had any real chance of success. Seen in those terms, the Europeans were people to be avoided and the Continent of Europe might be perceived as a continual source of trouble. While this misplaced view of Britain's European neighbours was serious enough in itself, the consequence of it appears to have been an unbalanced assessment of Britain's national interest. Above all, it appears to have misled successive governments, both Labour and Conservative, into believing that, if the notion of the three overlapping circles was indeed valid, the smallest and least important must be the one representing Europe.

There was one respect in which the UK displayed no reluctance to become involved in Europe. If Britain stood back from the European Coal and Steel Community and rejected the EEC, in a military sense no such reservations appeared to apply. The signing of the Treaty of Dunkirk, followed by the Treaty of Brussels the following year, confirmed that Britain was fully committed to sharing in the military defence of Europe. The next year (1949) saw the foundation of the North Atlantic Treaty Organisation (NATO) with the UK as one of the 12 founder members.

If Britain harboured political and economic doubts about the viability of partnership with Continental Europe, these clearly do not appear to have influenced military thinking at that time or subsequently. It is difficult to assess why this was the case. The possibility of invasion from Eastern Europe certainly appeared too real to ignore. A different factor may be that while Britain has declined in economic terms, its military influence has remained relatively unaffected. Between them, these two may shed some light on why the UK showed more enthusiasm for NATO than for the ECSC. They may also help to explain why, at least in one quarter, Britain was perceived as more interested in Anglo-American relations (the Americans being the dominant member in NATO) than in Europe.

Britain, the European Outsider

Few in Britain expected the plans for shared management of coal and steel to produce successful results. If few had expected the plan to succeed, an even smaller number expected that it would be likely to have an effect on the UK. Fewer still believed that the country would become a participant in the process.

In terms of production capacity, Britain had a significant lead over its European competitors. While the British attitude appeared essentially indifferent, if not negative, those countries actually involved recognised that

British membership would strengthen the emergent organizations. However, in the case of the ECSC (proposed by France in 1950), Britain
appeared highly sceptical, if not hostile. Britain had enjoyed a price
advantage in steel. Joint management of European steel industries might
have meant the erosion of that advantage.

It still appears unclear, even today, whether Britain simply refused to join
the Coal and Steel Community for reasons of its own, or whether the French
attitude at the time made British membership impossible. In reality, it matters
little now whether the UK cold-shouldered the ECSC or whether membership
was blocked by French opposition. Integrative structures began to develop
without British involvement and by the mid-1950s, there were signs that
Europe was becoming a more important factor in British calculations.

The six members of the ECSC soon resolved to take economic integration
a stage further by forming an Economic Community covering not merely the
strategically important commodities coal and steel but the whole range of
industrial goods. In addition, a common policy on agriculture was to be
developed, together with a common external tariff to apply to all goods
entering the Community from outside. Common administrative institutions
were to be set up.

Although the UK did take part in the negotiations for a short time, it
withdrew when it became clear that the likely outcome was not in line with
the British vision. One of many contentious issues was the proposal for a
common external tariff. British objections centred around the effect which
this could have on trading relations with Commonwealth countries.
However, this was hardly an insurmountable obstacle, as the example of
France shows. If France was able to secure an agreement which gave special
status to its overseas territories, then clearly a similar procedure could have
been adopted for the UK without too much difficulty.

The extension of the tariff-free movement of goods to cover agricultural
produce and the proposal for a common agricultural policy were both
viewed somewhat askance in the UK, which prided itself on the efficiency of
its agriculture and enjoyed relatively low food prices. To move in the
direction proposed would, it was argued, be detrimental to British interests
and would lead to imports of relatively expensive agricultural products from
Europe in place of the goods available from Commonwealth countries (such
as butter and lamb from New Zealand), which had traditionally received
preferential treatment.

It seems likely, however, that Britain also took exception to the creation
of European administrative institutions, such as a Council of Ministers, an
Assembly and a Commission. Britain had been instrumental in limiting the
powers of the Council of Europe, so it is unsurprising that the proposed EEC
institutional framework was considered unwelcome and unnecessary. This
attitude is best exemplified by the British counter-proposal for a free trade
area comprising the six members of the ECSC together with the other
members of the OEEC – some 17 states in all.

The free trade area envisaged by Britain would have had no common external tariff. Members were thus free to grant special privileges, as they saw fit. While internal tariffs on industrial products were to be removed, this did not apply to agriculture. There was to be no common agricultural policy, nor were there to be common administrative and political institutions. Such a structure did not provide for policy harmonisation in other areas, such as social welfare or economic management. This was tantamount to a *common market* based on the traditional British policy of free trade. Britain thus accepted the need for close trading relations with Europe, though other forms of integration were plainly not on the agenda.

To some extent, this approach might be described as *Realpolitik*. However, the example of the ECSC had proved that the "Continentals" were capable of organising themselves without British assistance and they were now ready to move a stage further. With the introduction of a common external tariff, British goods would be at a disadvantage in European markets at the very time when trading and other relations with Commonwealth states were beginning to erode.

In a number of ways, the free trade proposal was a genuine attempt to overcome British objections to the EEC and, as such, it was taken seriously, although the idea was ultimately rejected, largely due to French opposition. Nevertheless, it is an interesting reflection on the limited extent to which the British government of the day felt prepared to go. It could, of course, be argued in the light of developments since the mid-1980s that this position is still held by many influential politicians today.

Britain in opposition to Europe

The rejection of the free trade area left Britain with three alternatives. It could have opted to turn its back on the emergent EEC altogether and concentrated on its links with the Commonwealth and North America. A second option was to create an alternative organization to the EEC along similar lines to the free trade area, though with a much smaller membership in population terms. Finally, an application for EEC membership, whatever its potential difficulties, might have been made.

Of these, the second – the construction of an alternative structure – proved the most attractive. What emerged was the establishment of EFTA – the European Free Trade Association – comprising Britain, Norway, Sweden, Denmark, Portugal, Austria and Switzerland. These seven countries, as any map will confirm, were grouped around the periphery of the EEC and were sometimes referred to as the "outer seven".

Unlike the EEC, EFTA was, as the title suggests, simply a free trade area or common market with no real political dimension. It lacked the administration structures of the EEC, had no common external tariff and no common agricultural policy. There was also no commitment to "ever closer union" as envisaged in the Treaty of Rome; indeed in such an organization, this would have been virtually impossible. EFTA was clearly the made-in-Britain alternative to the EEC, designed to bring about the economic benefits of free trade but without the inherent drawbacks and political concessions. It might be argued that the creation of EFTA was in reality a peculiarly British response to a peculiarly British dilemma. As the largest state by far Britain could realistically expect to be the dominant force in EFTA both politically and economically. (The combined population of the other six, amounted to slightly more than half that of the UK). Had Britain become a member of the EEC at this juncture, it seems highly unlikely that it would have been able to exert the same degree of influence.

After agreement was reached on 20 November 1959, EFTA became operational on 1 January 1960. Having created an alternative to the EEC, however, Britain soon was contemplating membership. In July 1961, the MacMillan Government announced that an application for membership would be submitted to Brussels. Edward Health, then a minister in MacMillan's Cabinet, was given the task of negotiating the terms of entry. The choice of Heath was by any standards a wise one. Although there were many doubters in Parliament – and indeed in the country as a whole–Heath's commitment to Europe was beyond dispute. Heath did not share the narrow nationalistic attitude of some of his contemporaries and he firmly believed that membership would be beneficial to Britain.

The reasons for the change of heart in Westminster can be classed as political and economic. In the political sphere, it had become clear by this time that in global terms real power was held by the two military superpowers, the USA and the USSR. The Anglo-French experience during the Suez crisis in 1956 underlined the limited influence now exercised by individual European states – or even by two of the larger ones acting together. The extent to which this incident may have weakened the "special relationship" is not wholly clear.

What it does show, however, is that British interests by then could plainly no longer be automatically assumed identical to those of the USA and that in any conflict of priorities those of the latter would surely prevail. Moreover, it seems clear that American pressure was also a significant factor in hastening decolonisation.

The transformation of the British Empire into the Commonwealth signified a loosening of the administrative ties between overseas territories and the "mother" country. The wholesale granting of independence also meant that former colonies could no longer necessarily be expected to retain close economic and political ties with the UK. In a sense, the umbilical cord was being severed. Of Churchill's three overlapping circles, two can thus be seen as having declined in importance, while the third (Europe) was gradually gaining significance, as trading links with Europe expanded.

Britain, the Euro-applicant

Faced with the loosening of its ties with the Commonwealth and with a weakening of the "special relationship" with the USA. Britain arguably had valid reasons for turning to Europe, though this does not fully explain why an application for membership of the EEC was made.

From a British viewpoint, EFTA proved to be only a limited success at best. From an ideological standpoint, the EFTA arrangements overcame many British objections to the EEC, though in other respects it is surely true that the two were seriously mismatched. Although economically successful in their own right, countries such as Sweden and Austria lacked the pulling power of France or West Germany, while Portugal, although long an ally of Britain, lagged some way behind the West European average. In layman's terms, therefore, Britain in EFTA was a large fish in a rather small pond.

Had the EEC been seen to fail at this stage, then EFTA might have provided an adequate substitute. However, despite – or possibly because of – British non-participation, the EEC prospered. One implication of this was that in time the UK would become isolated economically. The common external tariff, once implemented, would apply to British goods, which would become less competitive in European markets.

In addition, it became clear that the performance of the British economy left much to be desired when compared to the economies of EEC members. Between 1958 and 1969, for example, real earnings in Britain grew by some 38% while the average increase in the EEC for the corresponding period was approximately 75%. There was thus a real danger that the UK would be left behind as well as isolated.

At first it appeared that the application would succeed, though ultimately, in January 1963, President de Gaulle announced his veto. Thereafter the application was withdrawn. In public at least, the reason for rejection appeared to be that Britain's "special relationship" with the USA was incompatible with a commitment to Europe. It is difficult to assess the validity of this with any accuracy without reference to a whole range of factors (such as the character of de Gaulle himself and his personal view of France's role in the world, his uneasy relations with both the Americans and the British and the *rapprochement* between France and West Germany to name but a few) which are outside the scope of this volume.

A second application by Harold Wilson's Labour government in 1966 met with rejection by de Gaulle the following year, though this time the application was left "on the table" to indicate that, as far as Britain was concerned, the matter was not yet considered closed. Nevertheless, no further progress was possible until after de Gaulle's retirement from politics. His successor, Georges Pompidou, let it be known that he had no opposition to British membership.

The General Election of 1970 returned the Conservative Party to power. Heath, the negotiator for the MacMillan Government in the early 1960s, now became Prime Minister and he succeeded where both Labour and Conservative administrations before him had failed. Talks began in June 1970 between the EC and four applicants in all. In addition to the UK, Norway, Denmark and the Republic of Ireland also had applied for membership.

The complex negotiation process lasted until 22 January 1972 when all four applicants signed a Treaty of Accession, to come into effect on 1 January 1973. Difficulties encountered included Commonwealth trade, the size of the British contribution to Community funds and fisheries policy, the latter with particular reference to the Norwegian application. As the major obstacle to British membership had previously been French opposition, Heath was careful to consult with President Pompidou (and with the West German Chancellor Willy Brandt) as a preparatory step.

Nevertheless, accession did little to allay misgivings about Europe – not least because the electorate had been given no say. The Labour Party, perceived as decidedly cool on Europe by many at the time, was returned to power in February 1974 having given a clear commitment to a national referendum on the issue. A referendum – the first in British constitutional history – was duly held the following year and produced a surprisingly large majority in favour of continued membership.

Britain, the uncomfortable member

Since accession in 1973, Britain's relationship with its European partners has remained uneasy in the main. The reasons for this are complex. While the pro-European lobby confidently expected economic benefits, many of these were slow to emerge, thus reflecting the fear of many anti-Europeans that Britain would be "dragged down" to the level of its partners. In reality, however, forces beyond the control of the UK – or indeed of the European Union as a whole – were responsible.

In the mid-1970s, for example, with the British economy barely recovering from the industrial unrest (typified by the three day week), which proved to be the undoing of the Heath Government, European economies as a whole experienced a period of recession. Following the Yom Kippur War in the autumn of 1973, oil-producing countries dramatically increased the price of crude oil while at the same time cutting production in order to "punish" the West for supporting Israel. As a result, the EC for the first time in its history experienced negative economic growth.

Two further periods of recession followed in the early 1980s and early 1990s, in which the UK suffered at least as badly as any of its European partners – arguably worse in some respects. Growing economic interdependence meant that all members were exposed to the same set of recessionary forces. A European trade cycle was emerging, in which all members experienced the same pressures at roughly the same time.

Logically, this would have required a co-ordinated programme of measures to combat the recession. However, particularly in the case of the UK and of France, governments chose to follow policies designed to produce a solution based on *domestic* priorities. If anything, this served to prolong the recessions in much the same way as government actions in the early 1930s sought national solutions to the global problems of the Great Depression.

If the UK had been a reluctant applicant, this reluctance has largely remained since becoming a member. It would, however, be facile to suppose that the British stance has been entirely negative. With good cause, Britain has, for instance, been active in campaigning for long overdue reforms of the Common Agricultural Policy and against fraudulent use of funds. Nevertheless, in the case of the former, the tone in which the campaign was conducted might, to put it gently, have been more diplomatic. As in the case of "Thatcher's Billion" , the style adopted was confrontational rather than co-operative. Britain's partners might, therefore, be forgiven for thinking that the UK takes an overly narrow nationalistic view of its place in Europe and that London is happiest when at odds with its partners.

On a more positive note, Britain was perhaps the most enthusiastic supporter of the Single European Market, the introduction of which removed the remaining barriers to the movement of goods, capital, people and services within the twelve member states. Similarly, Britain was active in supporting the creation of the European Economic Area, which incorporated the members of ETFA into the SEM. The British Presidency during the second half of 1992 saw substantial progress towards introduction of the deregulatory measures necessary for the implementation of the SEM. In addition, Britain professes to be one of the strongest supporters of enlargement of the EU. Britain can thus claim to have made a significant contribution to the development of the Union and to greater financial efficiency.

Nevertheless, in many respects the UK has found itself in opposition to its partners – often in a minority of one. It does not follow, of course, that the majority is always right and the minority always wrong. However, Britain's position has regularly been weakened by a reluctance to make concessions in order to secure general agreement. It may well be true, as Cabinet Ministers have often suggested, that other members share some of the concerns articulated by the UK, though, if this is the case, they seem singularly unwilling to provoke confrontation in defence of their interests.

With uncharacteristic enthusiasm Britain supported the Single European Market. At the same time, however, other measures contained in the same package met with total opposition, although the preamble to the EEC Treaty states quite unequivocally that its purpose was "to eliminate the barriers which divide Europe". In a sense, British opposition was somewhat disingenuous. It is difficult to believe that British politicians (some of whom had held ministerial office under Edward Heath!) were unaware of the wording of the Treaty or of its meaning. Had this been so, it is quite incredible that the Heath Government would have agreed to join. Nevertheless, many opponents of the social dimension attempted to create the impression that Britain had been tricked by a devious, overweening European Commission. In this, by any standards, they enjoyed a degree of success.

Specifically, Britain saw no need to introduce a uniform regime for wages, working conditions and employees' rights. Such measures can be seen as a logical requirement for the Single Market. Otherwise, employees will not really be free to take up employment anywhere in the Union without facing disadvantage or exploitation. Similarly, for the Single Market to function effectively, a single currency would arguably be valuable. Even free markets are likely to require some degree of regulation – if only to determine which practices are acceptable and which are not. The creation of unified conditions for trade within the EU also implied a need for closer union in other respects.

British support for the SEM mirrored almost exactly its opposition to political and monetary union and to the introduction of a harmonised social dimension. In the end, as Chapter Two shows, the Single Market, on which there was general agreement, was decoupled from the other measures in order to ensure its implementation. British opposition to the social dimension and the proposals for political and monetary union first became public at the Milan European Council in 1985, when Mrs Thatcher was scathingly dismissive of the whole idea. Throughout the remainder of the 1980s Conservative politicians, especially those on the right of the party, and much of the British press, continued their attacks. In some respects their criticism was plainly justified. A unified European policy on employee rights, for instance, would almost certainly prove cumbersome and bureaucratic.

However, instead of offering constructive alternatives, the British government chose to adopt a wholly negative approach based on ideological opposition to the principles involved. A "decency" wage, it was agreed, would destroy jobs and competitiveness. Proposals for a consultation regime would interfere with the "right to manage". The extension of fringe benefits and a degree of protection against unfair dismissal to many part-time employees would increase business costs and run counter to the notion of "flexibility". Britain much preferred, it was argued, to leave things as they were. Thus, instead of offering an alternative for discussion, Britain preferred simply to say no.

During her speech to the College of Europe in Bruges in 1988, Prime Minister Thatcher went as far as to ridicule the social dimension as "Socialism through the back door". Nevertheless, if the proposed regime was essentially Socialist in character, it is difficult to understand why mainstream European conservatives, such as Chancellor Kohl, appeared to have no problem whatsoever in accepting it. Similarly, if the social dimension would impose an unacceptable burden on businesses, why did this appear to be confined to the UK?

From a Euro-sceptic perspective it was none too difficult to portray the whole affair as an attempt to railroad Britain into accepting an alien European tradition and into surrendering precious British sovereignty to unelected and unaccountable bureaucrats in Brussels. In much the same way, it was argued that participation in a single European currency would have meant the end of the Pound Sterling and subjugation to the German Mark as its strongest consistent part.

As the European Commission proposed a non-binding Social Charter, British opposition continued. Although the Charter was, in effect, no more than a declaration of intent, the UK distanced itself from the idea. Similarly, when the Action Programme was proposed, Britain refused to sign. Unlike the Charter, the Action Programme contained concrete proposals, roughly half of which were legally binding. One of the objectives of the exercise was to make good practice – wherever it occurred – the standard. Where British practice was seen as meeting or exceeding the proposed minimum, no problems were encountered and Britain was happy to acknowledge praise. Where this was not the case, Britain was unwilling to act. As a result, when the proposals were put to the European Council for approval at Madrid in 1989, Britain alone of the twelve refused to agree. A compromise put forward by President Mitterrand at Strasbourg in late 1989 substantially weakened the package but even this concession was not sufficient to secure British agreement.

If the UK found the Social Charter (which was non-binding) unpalatable, it is not surprising that the Treaty on European Union (or Maastricht Treaty) provoked an even greater degree of hostility. While the Social Charter had made recommendations, the Social Chapter of the Treaty sought to transform these into legally binding commitments.

As is well known, Britain was eventually able to secure "opt-outs" from those parts of the Treaty which the Government found most objectionable – the Social Chapter and the final stage of the move towards a single currency. At the time, Prime Minister Major portrayed this as "game, set and match". Whether the "opt-outs" were a major victory for the UK or not is certainly debatable. For one thing, they sent a signal to the others in the EU that the UK set domestic – arguably even party political – considerations above broader European issues.

While political opponents of the Social Chapter publicly criticised proposals for a minimum wage and made dire predictions as to its potentially damaging effect on business activity, there appears to have been little real attempt to put the issues in perspective. Although real wages in the UK are low by European standards, the minimum under consideration would have affected only a relatively small number of wage earners in the UK. Predictions of large-scale job losses can thus be seen as unduly alarmist. It is also interesting to note that the most vehement objections to the Social Chapter were voiced not by the business community but by politicians. Conversely, support for such proposals from representatives ot organised labour appears to have been little more than lukewarm, suggesting thus that the proposed regime was somewhat less radical than its opponents claimed. What is true of the proposed minimum wage legislation probably applies in equal measure to other areas of the Social Chapter.

Opposition to the Maastricht Treaty also revolved around the apparent loss of sovereignty to individual states. It is ironic indeed that Britain, with one of the least devolved power structures in the western world, should take exception to the centralising tendencies of the EU and become the champions of subsidiarity in Europe.

How can the British stance be explained?

To a significant extent British attitudes have been coloured by a distinctive perception of the type of union which is considered politically acceptable. The idea of political integration, which involves a degree of shared sovereignty, would seem to imply a reduction in status, which many opponents of Europe cannot accept. To some extent this may derive from a lack of respect for our European partners, from a refusal to accept the UK's fall from grace, as it were.

It would also appear that the economic logic of closer ties had been easier to accept than the political dimension. It might be argued that all Britain has ever really wanted from Europe is a *common market* in the true sense. This might explain the original British proposal for a free trade area and the establishment of EFTA. Similarly, British support for the Single European market and for the creation of the EEA would be consistent with such a view. None of these implied a political commitment.

Rejection of the Social Charter and the Action Programme as well as of the Social Chapter of the Maastricht Treaty suggest that the UK's wish is to keep Europe at arm's length politically. To some extent this is understandable. The Thatcher Government professed to believe passionately in non-interventionist policies. On that basis, it is easy enough to construct a credible case against Brussels. However, much of the debate since the late 1980s has been couched in unacceptably narrow nationalistic and adversarial terms. This pandering to base instincts has been supplemented by blatant distortion. Although the EEC Treaty does contain a commitment to closer union, when this goal became an issue for debate after 1985 it tended to be portrayed in the press and by many Euro-sceptic politicians as a type of dirty trick dreamed up with the express purpose of upsetting the British.

Similarly, the distribution of power within the EU is often crassly misrepresented in the UK. The importance of the Council of Ministers, the real powerhouse, tends to be underplayed and the powers of the Commission exaggerated. The explanation for this may be that the UK has often been unable to present its case effectively in the Council of Ministers. Conservative critics, reluctant to embarrass a Conservative government over its failure in Council, have tended to shift the blame onto the Commission (which is not directly accountable) arguing that an all-powerful foreign bureaucracy is imposing alien and unwanted legislation on the UK. The Single European Act has given the Council of Ministers and the Parliament (in both of which the UK is represented with all mathematical fairness) an enhanced role in decision-making without giving more influence to the supposedly all-powerful Commission. Despite this, and despite wholehearted British support for the Single Market, distortions appear to go largely unnoticed – perhaps because they reflect widely held, if not necessarily accurate, beliefs.

The same might be said of British opposition to the social dimension of closer union. Proposals for a minimum wage regime or for the harmonisation of employee rights tend to be rejected on grounds of party ideology. While politicians may claim to speak on behalf of employers in this respect, it is noticeable that the employers themselves, while certainly not ecstatic, have said relatively little on the subject. In any event, Prime Minister Thatcher's description of the proposals as "Socialism through the back door" was in reality widely inaccurate. It is all but impossible to imagine how Chancellor Kohl, to name but one, could have supported any genuinely Socialist package of measures. The term Socialist should best be seen within the context of Thatcherite political vocabulary at the time and probably described ideas which Mrs Thatcher found unpalatable – not least because they ran counter to the policy of her Government. In reality, however, and although wage levels in the UK are plainly low by EU standards, only a relatively small number of employees in the UK would be affected by the introduction of a European minimum wage, though this has rarely been said in public. If the UK does not want to participate in full monetary union, the reasons advanced often seem to suggest that the decisive factor is emotional attachment to the Pound rather than the real difficulties which would arise. At the same time, little has so far been made of its advantages. In other words, genuine, informed debate has been rare.

From the above we can conclude that the UK seems to prefer a *common market* to European union and would prefer to keep Europe at arm's length both politically and economically; the UK remains an island off the north-west coast of the European mainland. Since the late 1940s surprisingly little has changed.

How European has the UK become?

Among EU members, voter turnout at European elections has been lowest in the UK with the exception of 1994. While some countries achieve high turnouts because voting is compulsory, the figures for the UK have tended to lag some way behind those where voting is voluntary. In point of fact, turnout for European elections in the UK is around half of that for

Westminster elections and not too far above the figures for local council elections. This would suggest that elections to Strasbourg are not seen as being of any great importance. Media coverage too is markedly less comprehensive than for general elections. It would appear that the British lack interest in, or awareness of, European issues. This is somewhat ironic, given repeated Euro-sceptic claims that European institutions are virtually all-powerful.

British lack of interest in things European is also reflected in other ways. As far as the ability to speak foreign languages is concerned, the UK's record is one of the weakest (though not the worst) in the European Union, as Figure 8.2 shows.

Figure 8.2 Percentage of adults claiming competence in European languages (selected EU countries)

	English	French	German	Italian	Spanish	Dutch/ Flemish
Belgium	26%	71%	22%	4%	3%	68%
Denmark	51%	5%	48%	1%	1%	1%
France	26%	100%	11%	8%	13%	1%
Germany	43%	18%	100%	3%	1%	3%
Ireland	99%	12%	2%	1%	1%	–
Italy	13%	27%	6%	100%	5%	–
Netherlands	68%	31%	67%	2%	4%	100%
Spain	13%	15%	3%	4%	100%	–
UK	100%	15%	6%	1%	2%	1%

(Source : P Gibbs : Doing Business in the European Community)

While many outside the UK are fluent in English and much business is conducted in English, this should not discourage British people (and Irish people, for that matter) from learning a European language. With the Single European Market now a reality, the need appears all the more urgent, if Britain is to benefit fully from the liberalisation of trading. To assume that only English is necessary might ultimately prove to be a serious handicap.

Similarly, the UK uses a different time to most of the European continent. An attempt to change this in the late 1960s ran into such opposition that it had to be abandoned. While this issue may be only of symbolic importance, it does mean that working hours in the UK are out of step with those of its

European partners. A British executive starting work at 9am might find that his French counterpart has already been at his desk for two hours. One hour of this may be due to the time difference and the second because the working day in France tends to begin earlier than in the UK. Similar anomalies could conceivably occur at the end of the day. Were the UK to adopt the same time as its partners, it would at the very least provide some evidence of a stronger commitment to Europe. The same might be said of driving on the left, although any change here would clearly be extremely costly and disruptive.

While such issues are largely symbolic, they do tend to reinforce the image of the UK as a country which stubbornly refuses to come to terms with its partners. There would be sound commercial reasons for using the same time as the majority in the EU, as this would increase the direct contact hours for businesses on both sides of the Channel. The use of a common time throughout the European Union would also make the transportation of goods easier to plan and it would probably also have a beneficial effect on tourism. A concession on the question of time might make it easier for the UK to secure accommodation from its partners in other areas where it feels that vital British interest are in jeopardy.

Perhaps the most important lesson to be learned from British opposition to the single currency and to the social dimension concerns not so much the validity of the proposals themselves as the UK's attitude to its partners. Above all what has emerged is a singular reluctance on the part of politicians to think European, to accept that there is more at stake than purely the interests of the UK – or sometimes the interests of a particular political party.

On this little appears to have changed. The Attlee Government rejected the ECSC for reasons which were to a significant extent party political. The same is true of the Thatcher and Major Governments over the social dimension of European union. While all the governments concerned were expressing a legitimate point of view, the way in which this was done suggests a distinct lack of enthusiasm or understanding for Europe. This does not mean that Britain should abandon opposition to those proposals which it dislikes. Instead it means that British governments should attempt to propose constructive alternatives by taking a more pro-active line. In many aspects the UK appears keener to safeguard its own priorities (which may be dictated by domestic party politics) and its British identity than it is on making a positive contribution to the future development of the EU. If the UK shows the will to work together with its partners, then its opinions will carry more weight.

Activity

☐ The chapter is devoted to Britain, so it is appropriate to consider Britain's attitude to your country.

☐ Of course, there is seldom a single opinion typical of a country as a whole. For example, the British perception of Germany or Japan may depend on the age of the respondent, with the younger generation taking a more positive view than their parents or grandparents.

☐ Therefore, you will need to look at various opinion groups in Britain in order to establish how they have reacted to your country over recent years.

☐ What factors could have influenced any changes you identify?

Chapter Nine

The Future

Aims of this chapter

□ To outline a range of issues which the EU will have to confront in the foreseeable future
□ To familiarise students with some possible solutions to the above
□ To follow contemporary trends in the EU
□ To identify other key issues and to offer possible solutions

While speculation about the future is notoriously dangerous, this chapter aims to give the reader insight into a number of issues, which are either problematic already or are likely to become so in the foreseeable future. Because the ultimate success of the EU may depend on how effectively these issues are tackled, simple solutions are offered for consideration, where this appears appropriate. Naturally, the definition of what constitutes a problem is easily influenced by the views of the observer. In much the same way, proposed solutions can be coloured unintentionally. Nevertheless, the authors attempt to present these in as neutral a way as possible. They make no claim that the list is exhaustive or that the order in which problems are presented is a reflection of their relative importance.

In many respects, the European Union can be considered a success. However, it would appear that the number of key issues will need to be resolved if it is to realise its goals and to develop satisfactorily in future years. These include: bureaucracy; the distribution of power; financial management; agreement on common policy objectives; membership; economic and social disparities, and foreign relations. Each of these general areas is considered in this chapter and some illustrative examples are given. It could, of course, also be argued that progress in other areas, such as security policy, is of equal importance. However, defence and security matters are outside the scope of this volume.

Bureaucracy

To many of its critics, it has become almost an article of faith that the EU is intensely bureaucratic and this view appears to be shared, at least to a limited extent, by some of its supporters. Euro-sceptics certainly appear to have little trouble in finding ammunition.

Administrative processes

To some extent, it may be inevitable that the EU is perceived in this way. The process of agreeing policy, drafting and preparing legislation for all 15 member countries is of necessity complex. Laws need to be translated into 11 working languages in such a way as to ensure that the meaning is identical. This process involves not merely the rendering of the actual words but also the need to take account of differing legal systems and practices. It is hardly surprising that the institutions of the European Union employ several thousand interpreters and translators. At the same time, it means that the actual law-making process will be both exacting and time-consuming. The complexity of the legislation itself is such that it must appear cumbersome. The Maastricht Treaty, in its English version, comprises over 60,000 words. Some Directives run to more than 30,000 words (by way of comparison, the American Declaration of Independence is some 1,000 words long).

Critics of the EU resent the fact that European law, where it exists, must take precedence over domestic legislation. This is particularly true of critics in the UK who find it relatively easy to portray EU institutions (most notably the European Commission) as slow-moving, heavy-handed and insensitive to national traditions. Sections of the tabloid process in the UK have on a number of occasions had some success in portraying Brussels as threatening quintessentially British institutions, such as sausages or ice cream, through the introduction of new laws.

The multi-national composition of the EU also means that the everyday business of institutions, such as the European Commission and the European Parliament, is conducted in all the working languages, into which all reports and other documents produced must be translated. In this sense too, the image of a cumbersome, slow-moving machine springs easily to mind. This is hardly helped, especially from a British perspective, by the persistence of the notion that Brussels is remote and unsympathetic.

Fewer languages?

As we have seen, part of the complexity arises from the use of so many working languages and if, as expected, membership continues to grow in coming years, the number of languages used is likely to increase. In theory, it might be possible to restrict the number of working languages which could lead to a simplification of many of the processes involved. While this may seem attractive at first glance, it could lay the EU open to charges of elitism. It would be difficult to resist using the languages of the larger and more powerful states and this could cause resentment among the smaller countries. The EU and its predecessors have thus far taken care to ensure that smaller members are not disadvantaged.

Remoteness

If the legislative process and the workings of the EU appear unwieldy, this may be at least partly because they are little understood. This in turn perpetuates the myth that individuals and organizations in the UK are powerless to exert any influence over decision-making and tends to reinforce resentment at the primacy of European law. In truth, however, the possibilities open to the UK in this regard are exactly the same as those open to the other 14 members. The nub of the problem is that the British seem unwilling or unable to avail themselves of the opportunities which exist.

The complexity of EU legislation has often given justifiable cause for concern. To simplify instruments such as Directives would thus appear to be an attractive idea which would help to counter the view that Europe is too bureaucratic. It is debatable whether this can be achieved without comprising, at least to some extent, the principle of universal application and interpretation. If it is true that the workings of European institutions remain relatively impenetrable, this could be countered by better management of information – perhaps through the release of widely circulated reports or briefings, explaining key developments in terms readily understandable to the non-specialist.

While it is easy to sympathise with those who claim that the European Union is too bureaucratic, the establishment of the Single European Market from 1 January 1993 suggests that attempts are being made to address aspects of the problem. A major feature of the SEM is the removal of bureaucratic restrictions to the movement of goods, capital, labour and services. The UK Presidency (in the second half of 1992) contributed a great deal towards simplification and deregulation. One example of what has been achieved with the establishment of the SEM is the introduction of the Single Administrative Document covering the movement of goods within the European Union. What this shows is that it is perfectly possible to devise processes and documents which require less paperwork than before and should therefore prove less time-consuming. Whether this will in itself be sufficient to change attitudes in the UK remains a moot point, however. It seems more likely that Europe's image in the UK will only begin to improve significantly when government adopts a more pro-active stance.

The distribution of power

In addressing this issue, as with that of bureaucracy, it is not easy to separate peculiarly British perceptions from questions affecting the EU as a whole.

The Council of Ministers

One issue which illustrates this concerns decision-making in the Council of Ministers. As membership has grown, it has proved increasingly difficult to achieve unanimity (however desirable this may be). Partly as a result of this and partly as a result of the Single European Act, Qualified Majority Voting, as described in Chapter Three, has been used on a growing number of issues. Membership of the EU grew to 15 on 1 January 1995 and further accessions are to be expected in coming years.

This raises two questions. Firstly, the size of the blocking minority (23 weighted votes prior to the accession of Austria, Finland and Sweden on 1 January 1995) will need to be revised as new members join. Second, with further growth in membership to be expected, unanimity is likely to prove even more difficult to achieve in future. It seems that the number of issues requiring unanimity will have to be reduced and that even more decisions than at present will be taken by simple majority or by Qualified Majority Voting. Thirdly, it also seems likely that, with expanded membership, the length of time required for decision-making in the Council of Ministers will increase unless the number of issues requiring unanimity is reduced.

While such changes are easily justifiable on objective grounds, Euro-sceptics in the UK have tended to portray the reduction in the number of decisions requiring unanimity as an erosion of a specifically British right of veto. However, the reality is that no member has ever possessed such an exclusive right. In any event, if the UK thus now has fewer opportunities to veto unpalatable proposals, the same applies in exactly the same way to the other 14!

Leaving Euro-sceptic objections to one side, it is difficult to envisage what alternatives there are to increased use of QMV. Here too, the adoption of a more pro-active stance by the UK might ultimately prove more useful than continued negative campaigning from the sidelines.

A further difficulty concerns the power exercised by the Council of Ministers itself. As we have seen, the Council is the real powerhouse of the European Union, where the most important decisions are taken and where most real power lies. If it is possible to argue that the Commissioners and their staff are not sufficiently accountable, the same could be said of ministers participating in the Council. While they may resign from office or lose office after electoral defeat in their home countries, there is no European machinery for their removal and they are not really accountable to anyone on a European level. While it is, of course, true that they represent national governments, they do have the power to overrule or disregard decisions taken by the Commission or the Parliament. A degree of European accountability would therefore seem appropriate. Parliament, as we have seen, has the power to dismiss the Commissioner. It must be worth considering whether the Council of Ministers could be made accountable to Parliament in Strasbourg.

Subsidiarity or centralisation

Many of the objections voiced by the UK to what it sees as the excessive federalism of Europe revolve round the notion of subsidiarity. While this term is by no means easy to define, it can be taken to mean that decisions should, wherever possible, be made at the lowest practical level in a hierarchical sense. In other words, the less power there is concentrated at the centre the better. Subsidiarity has become a crucial argument in the British case against the perceived loss of sovereignty to Brussels.

However, it is difficult to understand why the UK with its extremely centralised domestic power structure, which allows little autonomy to the regions, should urge the European Union to devolve power away from the centre. It would appear that Britain's commitment to subsidiarity owes more to government's desire to block the process of deepening within the European Union than it does to any real and lasting commitment to the devolution of power.

Central to much of this is the reality that, whatever the actual distribution of institutional power, some decisions will inevitably have to be taken at the centre. The key to the resolution of the issue is the need to achieve agreement on what power *must* be held at the centre and what can safely be devolved. It is, therefore, highly ironic that the UK, with massive concentration of power in Westminster, should be projecting itself as the advocate of devolution in Europe. From a European perspective it might thus appear that the UK is applying double standards. Alternatively, it could be argued that the British stance during the late 1980s and early 1990s in some ways mirrors London's refusal to participate in the single currency. In other words, it can be seen largely as an emotional response.

The European Parliament

Contrary to some perceptions, the European Parliament currently exercises relatively little real power. Paradoxically, of all the EU institutions, the Parliament is by far the most obviously accountable, as its members are directly elected by the voters every five years. As we have seen, the EP lacks the right to initiate legislation, other than in budgetary matters. While the idea of extending the legislative powers of Strasbourg may seem an obvious solution, this may well prove highly problematic unless balanced by the creation of European institutions of a truly governmental nature. In any event, Euro-sceptics and anti-Federalists can hardly be expected to be enamoured of the idea.

It might be possible to give the EP the final say on legislation (in much the same way as Parliament in the UK) rather than the Council of Ministers as at present. However, this would probably mean the introduction of a third reading of proposed laws, and this would almost certainly result in a slowing down of a decision-making process, which may already be both cumbersome and time-consuming.

The European Parliament already has the power, under certain conditions, to dismiss all Commissioners. In terms of accountability, this is clearly a significant function. It might, therefore, be logical to suggest that the EP could be given a say in the choice of Commissioners.

At present, these are nominated by national governments and it seems appropriate that this element of national input should be retained, not least because to remove it would serve to reinforce the notion that the Commission is remote and unaccountable. In future Commissioners might conceivably be chosen from nominations put forward by individual countries, subject to parliamentary approval. Just as a two-thirds majority is presently required in order to secure the removal of the Commission *en bloc*, Parliament might be given the power to veto nominations subject to a two-thirds majority.

Under present arrangements, many individuals feel remote from the European Parliament. While this may be a geographical problem, it also suggests that many (not least in the UK) find it difficult to understand the EP and its work. If, as seems possible, the EP acquires more power, then this issue will need to be addressed. During each member's tenure of the Council Presidency, it might make sense to relocate at least two plenary sessions of the European Parliament to that country. One of these could perhaps be timed to coincide with the meeting of the European Council. In this respect, it could also be worth considering whether these sessions of the EP might be held outside the capital city or the city in which the national Parliament normally sits. In this way, the EP would not be associated with the structures of political power in member states or with the problems associated with the over-concentration of power at the centre. This idea is hardly new. If European Councils have been held in Maastricht and Birmingham – to name but two locations outside capital cities – then the principle might be applied to Parliamentary sessions as well. It would have the added benefit of strengthening links between the regions and the institutions of the Union. The Parliament also has representative offices in each of the member states of the European Union, which could be used as a channel of communication and for publicising this work and responsibilities.

National and regional identities have been a key issue in European affairs since the process of integration began in the early post-war years. This can be taken to mean that diversity is perceived as one of Europe's strengths and therefore worth preserving. At the same time, this would seem to imply that it is important to allow countries and regions the greatest possible say over decisions which affect them directly and thus a clear stake in the future of the union. One problem with this concerns the distribution of political power within individual member states. While the German constitution, for instance, allows the Länder a substantial degree of autonomy, it is difficult to imagine how this could be implemented across the EU as a whole – especially in countries such as the UK where virtually all real power has traditionally been concentrated at the centre. On the other hand, the Maastricht Treaty contains a clear commitment to the preservation of diverse practices wherever possible. Closer political union thus would appear to imply a compromise on this issue, though the actual detail of such an arrangement is difficult to imagine.

Electoral arrangements

Although the Treaty of Rome makes provision for common arrangements concerning elections to the European Parliament, this goal has yet to be achieved. One reason may be that responsibility for the introduction of any common electoral system rests with the Council of Ministers, the institution in which the national interest of members is most clearly represented. As things stand, 14 of the 15 EU members use variants of Proportional Representation (PR) for elections to Strasbourg, the exception being the UK.

In effect, it matters little, if at all, what system is actually used for the purpose and what the merits of different systems are. Agreement on a common system of translating votes into seats would, at the very least, give a greater semblance of unity to the process. Similarly, this would be reinforced, if all members could agree to hold the elections on the same day or days – say, on a Sunday or over Saturday and Sunday, when most voters would not be at work. It is indeed ironic that votes are actually counted (and results announced) at roughly the same time. This being so, it ought to be possible to reach an agreement acceptable to all on the scheduling of the poll and on the modalities of the electoral system itself.

The European Commission

Of the major institutions, the European Commission appears to be the most remote and is the most often criticised for that reason. One way in which this could be addressed might be by devolving much of the work currently performed in Brussels to branch offices distributed throughout the Union. This would seem to bring the Commission closer to the people actually affected by its work and would be a visible sign of their stake in the decision-making process. A further significant benefit of such devolution would be that the Commission "Head Office" in Brussels would then be better able to concentrate its efforts on broad issues affecting the EU as a whole. It should, therefore, be better placed to perform a more effective co-ordinating role. Moreover, this would clearly be more in keeping with the Commission's self-image as the conscience of the Union and the guardian of the European ideal. Nevertheless, this is far from unproblematic. For one thing, it would appear to add an extra layer of bureaucracy to an institution which many already feel to be too bureaucratic. For another, it seems likely that of the devolved functions and responsibilities some will be perceived as more prestigious, and therefore more desirable, than others.

Financial management

If the EU is often perceived as remote, cumbersome and bureaucratic, it has also (and with some justification) been perceived as wasteful in its use of financial resources and as weak in the management of its financial affairs.

Agriculture

The Common Agricultural Policy (CAP) is usually seen as the prime example of wasteful expenditure – not least because it accounts for over 60% of the EU's budget. To its numerous critics the CAP is to blame for chronic over-production (of which butter mountains and wine lakes are among the best known symbols), for high food prices in the shops and for apparently rewarding small, relatively inefficient, farming units through its system of subsidies. Ironically, the CAP can even make payments to farmers who take agricultural land out of production in order to remain within quotas.

On the credit side, some positive achievements should also be recorded. Thanks largely to the CAP, food shortages in EU countries have been all but eliminated and modernisation has taken place on a substantial scale. It may also be true that the CAP has reduced the number of bankruptcies in the agricultural sector, though certainly without eliminating them altogether.

Nevertheless, a balanced view must surely be that the CAP has probably created at least as many problems as it has solved – and that it has been the source of much unnecessary friction within the EU and between the EU and its trading partners elsewhere. A solution is far from easy to envisage. To make substantial cuts in subsidies, as suggested by the United States during the Uruguay Round of the GATT negotiations, may seem economically prudent. It would also lead to freer competition for agricultural produce on a global scale. However, it might not be politically wise to do so, given the influence wielded by farmers throughout most of the EU. Reduced subsidies would almost inevitably lead to bankruptcies on a considerable scale in the agricultural and related sectors and therefore to a rise in unemployment. Clearly unemployment could have political consequences for those in power. Moreover it would create the need to generate job opportunities for those made redundant.

To take no action would scarcely be acceptable. Above all, it would merely serve to reinforce the already common view that the CAP is no more than a scheme which rewards inefficient agricultural units at the expense of others. The need for resolution appears all the more urgent if membership of the Union is to increase. It seems fairly likely that before too long former Communist states in Central and Eastern Europe, where agriculture is perceived as notoriously inefficient, will apply for membership. The likely impact of this on an unreformed CAP is hardly an attractive prospect.

Fraud

A report published by the Court of Auditors in November 1994 suggested that large-scale fraud is endemic in the EU. There is no shortage of anecdotal (and other) evidence that EU funds are being used for fraudulent purposes. One infamous example concerned the payment of subsidies under the Common Agricultural Policy for the cultivation of non-existent olive trees. It is, of course, proper that the Court of Auditors should draw attention to such abuses, though this is perhaps akin to the discovery of irregularities in a company's accounts at the end of the financial year. The crucial question is whether this should have been spotted earlier.

Responsibility for the day-to-day management of the EU's finances rests with the European Commission, which in turn is answerable to Parliament. In the Commission's defence it should be said that with a relatively small staff and with limited financial resources of its own, there are clear limits to what can be achieved. It might be realistic to give the Commission wider powers of investigation together with greater resources in order to ensure that EU finances are managed effectively. Close co-operation with national and regional authorities, to whom certain powers might conceivably be devolved, would also be indispensable.

If part of the Commission's work was devolved to regional offices, as suggested earlier, these could play a major role in investigating fraud. While this could cause a degree of resentment, all EU members ultimately would wish to see the best possible management of EU funds (which stem after all from taxpayers' contributions). On balance, such an approach would surely prove acceptable, especially if offenders were subject to tough penalties.

Financial transactions

The introduction of the Single Market has meant a substantial degree of deregulation through the removal of legal and other restrictions on the movement of goods and capital. While this clearly benefits legitimate trade, membership. For the most part, membership is perceived as beneficial, although doubts have been voiced often enough, particularly in the UK and in Denmark. On the other hand, it seems likely that Greece, Portugal and Spain in particular have gained more than most from membership in at least one respect. All three of the above have found themselves relatively isolated from the European mainstream, politically and to a large extent also economically, while under authoritarian rule. Membership of the EC/EU has helped to end this isolation and appears to have strengthened the countries' commitment to the maintenance of democratic institutions.

Potential new members in Mediterranean Europe

Prospective applicants such as Malta, Cyprus and Turkey may be peripheral to Europe in a geographical sense, though they too would undoubtedly benefit from accession. In the case of Turkey, the country's recent record on human rights might well prove a major obstacle to membership. It also remains to be seen whether Greece would be comfortable with the prospect of Turkish membership.

Eastern Europe

Following the momentous events of 1989–1990, which brought about the end of Cold War structures in Europe, it now seems likely enough that former Communist states will wish to accede to the EU. In the shorter term, the most obvious candidates would probably be Hungary and the Czech Republic. Eventually Polish, and perhaps even Russian, membership cannot be ruled out altogether.

Such developments would clearly be welcome in many ways, not least because, as in the case of Spain, Greece and Portugal, it would demonstrate that these countries were no longer isolated from the European mainstream. However, their accession to the European Union is likely to prove somewhat problematic. One reason for this concerns their general level of prosperity, which presently falls well below the EU average. Early accession would thus put an additional strain on the EU's finances, as all of the above would almost inevitably be net beneficiaries. Furthermore, the potential effect of the Common Agricultural Policy will need to be assessed carefully, given the reputation for inefficiency, even by present European Union standards, of agriculture in these countries.

The EFTA rump

The status of the remaining EFTA members (Switzerland, Iceland, Norway and Liechtenstein) may also prove a difficult issue. Economically, it would seem logical enough for all of these to accede to the EU, though this may be nullified by political considerations.

The Norwegian electorate has already rejected accession on two occasions – apparently in response to concerns about a potential loss of independence. While the issue of EU membership has not yet been put to Swiss voters, their rejection of the EEA would seem to indicate that their response to the EU would be similar. The Swiss people, rather like the Norwegians, appear to prize their country's independence more highly than any economic benefits likely to occur from accession. Moreover, the Swiss tradition of strict neutrality in international affairs may not be easily reconciled with the demands of membership. Many in Switzerland might feel that their high living standards could be compromised if the country joins the European Union. Interestingly enough, similar arguments about the potential threat to living standards were advanced in the UK by opponents of Europe when the question of accession was first widely debated in the UK.

Widening or deepening?

In general the European Union welcomes applications from prospective members, though in many cases transitional arrangements are necessary (as, for example in the case of Portugal and Spain) in order to achieve the necessary degree of synchronisation.

As far as extended membership is concerned, the UK has taken the line that new members are welcome. However, this process (often referred to as "widening") also creates problems connected with the pace at which the EU can progress towards closer union (or "deepening"). It might be argued that Britain is especially keen to encourage widening because this can be used as a lever to slow down – if not stop altogether – the deepening process.

In future years, it seems likely that, while transitional arrangements will still be required, new members may well have less scope than the UK currently enjoys to retard progress, thus leaving Britain still relatively isolated. In any event extended membership raises the question whether newcomers will be able (both politically and economically) to move forward at the same pace as longer-established members. This may well increase the likelihood of a two-speed Europe, though whether the UK finds itself in the "slow lane" will surely be a question more of political will than the country's suitability.

Economic and social disparities

A key objective of the Treaty of Rome was, as we have seen, the reduction of economic and social disparities. To this end, the European Union has a number of mechanisms at its disposal, such as the Regional Development Fund and the Social Fund. The notion of "cohesion" is now firmly embedded in EU policy. However, as visible imbalances remain, the question arises as to how successful the policy has actually been.

The relative prosperity of individual members will determine the level of the contribution they make to EU funds. In the case of the UK it would appear that the original assessment made was probably too optimistic, hence the disputes of the late 1970s and early 1980s over the overall level of the British contribution. The only equitable basis for contributions is surely the notion that the more prosperous states pay more (becoming net contributors), while the less fortunate pay less (becoming net beneficiaries). It is perhaps only natural that net contributors will feel that they pay too much. With the possible accession of relatively impoverished countries from Central and Eastern Europe, this problem is likely to be exacerbated.

The Maastricht Treaty

The Social Chapter of the Maastricht Treaty aims to create a level playing field within all member states of the EU by harmonising minimum standards for employee rights, wages and other aspects of employment conditions. This can be justified in terms of the Treaty of Rome, which contains a commitment, albeit somewhat vaguely expressed, to that effect. It can also be argued that if the Single European Market (notably freedom of movement for labour) is to function properly then employees must be able to move from one country to another without experiencing disadvantage. The UK has regularly opposed harmonisation in this area. Part of the argument is that measures of this type are likely to prove bureaucratic and difficult to enforce. It is certainly none too difficult to sympathise with such a view in the light of past performance. However, British objections also appear to be politically motivated.

The British stance

British Government policy in the second half of the 1980s appeared to be heading in the opposite direction to that of Europe. While proposals for a minimum wage regime were being considered in Brussels, Britain removed statutory protection for those in the lowest paid jobs. Similarly, while deregulation in the UK appeared to erode the rights of employees, European proposals designed to create a minimum acceptable standard for the EU were resolutely opposed by London. British objectors to the social dimension often argue that what is required is a "flexible" labour market. The flexible market appears to be based on a negation of the principles behind the Commission's Social Charter and the Social Chapter of the Maastricht Treaty. The British case appears to revolve around potential increased costs to employers and the erosion of the right to manage. Ironically, if reactions from the European Union as a whole are considered, this would only appear to be a problem in the UK.

If British concerns are shared by many others, as Cabinet Ministers claim, it seems inexplicable that they are not prepared to say so in public. After all, other EU governments such as that of France, have been active enough at different times in the defence of vital interests. If British doubts are indeed widely shared, then it seems strange that the negotiation of "opt-outs" has not been much more widespread – especially if, as claimed, this is tantamount to "game, set and match".

It would appear, however, that the "flexible" labour market in reality means that the balance of power in industrial relations would be somewhat one-sided. This may explain why the view is not held by the majority in the EU – or indeed even by mainstream European conservatives. In any event, there does not appear to be any hard evidence that the "flexible labour market" in the UK will attract jobs from elsewhere in the EU. Similarly, it is probably impossible to prove that the opposite approach destroys jobs. In this connection, it is interesting to note that the most pessimistic predictions are made by Euro-sceptic politicians in the UK rather than by employers, who would stand to lose most, if the view is correct.

It is far from easy to predict how this issue might be resolved. On balance, given the weight of opinion in the EU, it seems likely that the majority view will prevail and that Britain will ultimately have to soften its opposition. New members, moreover, are likely to enjoy less scope for the articulation of dissent than the UK currently has.

Foreign relations

While it could be argued that an organization such as the European Union would have a clear need for an agreed foreign policy, it would appear from what has emerged so far that an effective foreign policy remains a distant prospect. The failure of the EU to have any real impact on the situation in Bosnia will serve as an example. While it is true that the EU has had some success in Bosnia (for example with humanitarian aid), this falls well short of what might be achieved. Part of the explanation for this may be that for many EU members (especially in foreign affairs) national priorities still take precedence. European policy can best be defined perhaps only in outline. Over 130 countries now have separate diplomatic relations with the European Union. While it is tempting to portray this as a foreign policy success, in reality it only provides proof of international recognition not that policy has been successful.

Conclusion

Although substantial progress has been made in many areas (such as the Single European Market and in the expansion of membership), the European Union still has many weaknesses. It is perceived as bureaucratic, wasteful and somewhat remote – especially by its critics in the UK. Moreover, despite its title, the organization appears less than unified in many policy areas. This may be because its members still tend to think in national rather than European terms.

Activity

☐ This is probably the most difficult area for an activity, as constant changes in world events influence the behaviour of individual countries.

☐ There are always problems in the world, and it is the current events that you can address.

☐ Try to estimate the contribution your country would make to solving – or intensifying – these problems.

Selected Bibliography

Archer, C., *Organising Western Europe*, Edward Arnold, 1990

Barnes, I., Davison, L. (eds) *European Business Text and Cases*, Butterworth-Heinemann, 1994

Barnes, I., Preston, J., *The European Community*, Longman, 1990

Cecchini, P., *The European Challenge*, Wildwood House, 1988

Corbett, R., Jacobs, F., *The European Parliament*, Longman, 1991

Dutton, D., *British Politics Since 1945*, Blackwell, 1991

George, S., *Britain: An Awkward Partner in the EC*, OUP, 1990

George, S., *Politics and Policy in the European Community*, (2nd ed.), OUP, 1991

Gibbs, P., *Doing Business in the European Community*, Kogan Page, 1993

Joll, J., *Europe since 1870, an International History*, Penguin, 1983

Kent, P., *European Community Law*, M&E, 1992

Keohane, R., Hoffman, S. (eds), *The New European Community, Decision Making and Institutional Change*, Westview, 1991

Kirchner, E., *Decision-making in the European Community*, Manchester University Press, 1992

Minford, P. (ed.), *The Cost of Europe*, Manchester University Press, 1992

Nicoll, W., Salmon, T., *Understanding the European Communities*, Philip Allan, 1990

Nugent, N., *The Government and Politics of the European Community*, Macmillan, 1993

Owen, R., Dynes, M., *The Times Guide to the Single European Market*, Times Books, 1993

Perry, K., *Business and the European Community*, Butterworth-Heinemann, 1994

Pinder, J., *European Community*, OUP, 1991

Randlesome, C. et al, *Business Cultures in Europe*, (2nd ed.), Butterworth-Heinemann, 1993

Roney, A., *The European Community Fact Book*, (3rd ed.), Kogan Page, 1993

Spero, J., *The Politics of International Economic Relations*, (4th ed.), Routledge, 1992
Swann, D., *The Economics of the Common Market*, (7th ed.), Penguin, 1992
Tayeb, M., *The Global Business Environment*, Sage, 1992
Vadney, T., *The World Since 1945*, (2nd ed.), Penguin, 1992
Walsh, L., *International Marketing*, M&E, 1993
Weigall, D., Stirk, P., *The Origins and Development of the European Community*, Leicester University Press, 1992
Young, J., *Cold War Europe 1945–1989*, Arnold, 1991

Index